Worship:

True worship is the mind and heart humbly focusing upon the Sovereign Living Lord Jesus Christ as He is revealed in the Word of God. Whenever that happens, there will be an inner falling down before Him in both surrender and praise.   – *Page 91*

Witness:

Effective evangelism results from overflow—the overflow of the Holy Spirit from the life of the Spirit-filled believer, thus revealing to others the reality of the indwelling Christ.   – *Page 116*

Warfare:

When you pray according to God['s Word, you] pray according to God's will. And it [is then possible] for you to know victory over Sa[tan's every] attempt to derail your spiritual life.

Food for Faith

Food for Faith

A Biblical Manual
**Guidelines for a consistent and
living fellowship with God**

Richard A. Bennett

Cross Currents International Ministries
Dallas, Texas

Printed in the United States of America

Library of Congress Catalog Card Number: 98-67798

ISBN: 1-57736-113-X

Scripture quotations are from *The New King James Version*—1979, 1982,
Thomas Nelson, Inc., Publishers. Used by permission.

Scripture quotations marked NIV are from *The Holy Bible, New International
Version*—1973, 1978, 1984, International Bible Society. Used by permission.

Scripture quotations marked Amp are from *The Amplified New Testament*—
The Lockman Foundation 1954, 1958. Used by permission.

Scripture quotations marked KJ are from *The King James Version. All scriptures
are in italics.*

Photo courtesy of Verlag Klopfenstein, Adelboden

Published by
Cross Currents International Ministries
P.O. Box 551144
Dallas, Texas 75355-1144

Distributed by
International Prison Ministry
P.O. Box 130063
Dallas, Texas 75313

In the Name of our Lord Jesus Christ, this book is affectionately dedicated to every co-laborer who has so faithfully labored with my wife and me in the ministry of the Gospel through Cross Currents International Ministries.

Food for Faith is already printed in other languages as a missionary extension of Cross Currents International Ministries and International Prison Ministry. Further missionary translations and printings are pending.

Contents

Foreword

It is a privilege to commend Dr. Richard A. Bennett's new title, *Food for Faith*. It is a worthy sequel to his earlier book *Your Quest for God*. Man cannot come to God without faith *(Hebrews 11:6)* and he cannot live for God without faith *(Romans 1:17)*. For this to be possible faith must be **fed** both initially *(Romans 10:17)* and continually *(1 Peter 2:1-3; Hebrews 5:12-14)*. The Lord Jesus finalized the matter when He declared, *Man shall not live by bread alone, but by every word that proceeds from the mouth of God (Matthew 4:4)*. Earlier Jeremiah confirmed this principle when he wrote, *Your words were found, and I ate them, and Your word was to me the joy and rejoicing of my heart; for I am called by Your name, O Lord God of hosts (Jeremiah 15:16)*.

For maximum benefit, spiritual food must be **appreciated, appropriated and then assimilated**. Dr. Bennett shows us how this process takes place in our times of 'togetherness' with God. Chapter 8, in particular, is most helpful in this regard.

In a day of secular humanism, when the average Christian has been brainwashed to think that he can live for God without total **faith-dependence** on the indwelling Christ (*Galatians 2:20*), a book like *Food for Faith* is a message from Heaven to all of us. May God bless the ministry of this book as it goes forth on its mission.

Dr. Stephen F. Olford
Memphis, Tennessee

Preface

FOOD FOR FAITH is really the sequel to *Your Quest for God*, a book I wrote when my wife and I approached our twenty-fifth wedding anniversary. At that time, we wanted to express our thanksgiving to God by writing, printing and publishing this earlier presentation of the Gospel message.

The first printing of *Your Quest for God* was twenty-five thousand copies. Since then, God has seen fit to bless our simple love offering to Him in a most remarkable way.

Today, approximately three million copies have been distributed around the world in over fifty languages, and the demand for this book continues to grow dramatically. Among our greatest joys has been to hear accounts of people who have been born again in many parts of the world as the result of reading this book.

Later we were about to celebrate our thirty-fifth wedding anniversary! During the intervening years, doors opened to the gospel and therefore to the distribution of *Your Quest for God* in ways that we could never have conceived of ten years before. Consequently, we could think of no better way to express our growing love and gratitude to our Heavenly Father than by printing and publishing *Food for Faith*. Even as God has blessed *Your Quest for God*, may He also use this second book to help the many people who are finding new life in Christ, both here and in countries around the world.

However, *Food for Faith* is not just a sequel to *Your Quest for God*. Dorothy and I believe that it will, in and of itself, become a vital help to every believer who desires a more intimate relationship with the Lord. It was written with the sincere prayer that each person who reads it will find special help and encouragement in his or her Christian life.

Food for Faith is not really intended to be read in a casual way. Neither is it meant to be read and then laid aside. After it has been read carefully, it should be kept handy as a reference manual. As the principles in this book are faithfully applied to our lives, we will learn how to develop a more consistent and intimate walk with God.

Many of us consider it wise to have an occasional medical 'check-up'. To do this we invest money and a little time. The correct diagnosis of any physical problem, and its subsequent treatment, will greatly depend on the initial questions the doctor asks. It is also wise for Christians to have an occasional spiritual 'check-up'. And all that this requires is transparent honesty and the investment of time as we draw aside to be alone with God! At the end of each chapter, a few helpful questions are suggested as the basis of your own personal 'Spiritual Check-up'. Some of these questions might make you feel uncomfortable. Please remember that in a physical examination the place where it is too painful to probe is generally the place where the problem lies!

In writing this book I have been reminded of an incident which was told to me by my friend, the late Dr. J. Edwin Orr. He said that a well-known speaker had been invited to join with him and other selected Christian leaders in an important national gathering which had been convened exclusively for the purpose of intercessory prayer. However, the unnamed speaker to whom Edwin referred, graciously declined the invitation and explained that he was too busy to attend the protracted prayer meetings. At the same time, he added an appendage to his letter of refusal in which he stated that he had a very good message about prayer and would be pleased to come and preach it at any such subsequent gathering! My heart is only too well aware how much easier it is to write or preach about prayer than it is to really pray. So I write not as a specialist, but as one hungry person telling other hungry people where they can find bread.

My wife Dorothy has not only been a great encourager in my writing of *Food for Faith*, but even more importantly she has consistently sought to guard and encourage my time alone with God. How clearly I remember having read one of C. T. Studd's prayers, which, before I met Dorothy, I also prayed. It went something like this: "Lord, if you have a wife for me, let her be a red hot poker spurring me on when I am tempted to let up!" What a privilege it has been to have been married to such a wife. Praise God!

It is now over fifty years since my father-in-Christ, Dr. Stephen Olford, led me to the Savior. I am so thankful that at that time Stephen also shared with me the supreme importance of a regular time of Bible reading and prayer.

Many of the thoughts expressed in this book spring from my personal reflection on God's Word. Other truths have been gleaned from the biblical insights of many choice servants of God whom the Lord has graciously brought across my path. Although these faithful men and women are too numerous to identify in the context of a small and practical publication such as this, for each and every one I praise the Lord.

Now, through the publishing of *Food For Faith*, I can, in turn, obey the injunction that Paul gave to his son in the faith, Timothy: *And the things that you have heard from me among many witnesses, commit these to faithful men who will be able to teach others also (2 Timothy 2:2).*

Though this book was written to help believers enjoy a consistent fellowship with the Lord Jesus, there will be those reading these pages who have not as yet come to know the joy of sins forgiven and the marvelous assurance of eternal life. If you are such a person, I urge you to turn in your Bible to the gospel of John. There you will read why this gospel can be of special help to you: *But these are written that you may believe that Jesus is the Christ, the Son of God, and that believing you may have life in His name (John 20:31).*

– R.A.B.

Food
for
Faith

How sweet are Your words to my taste,
Sweeter than honey to my mouth! . . .
Therefore I love Your commandments
More than gold, yes, than fine gold!

Psalm 119:103, 127

CHAPTER 1

Daily Delight

A short while ago a very gracious Christian lady earnestly requested: "Please pray that I might have a more intimate relationship with the Lord." Yes there are different degrees of intimacy in any interpersonal relationship. And that is particularly true for Christians in their relationship with the Lord Jesus Christ.

Even in human relationships, the true togetherness of emotional ties can only blossom when accompanied by a blending of wills; a sharing of value systems; an enjoyment of common interests; an honesty of open communication, and a meeting of the minds.

For example, my wife Dorothy and I recently received a letter which brought us both tremendous joy. It came from two Africans. It read: "Yesterday we brought baby Dorothy home from the hospital; like her namesake, she decided to be punctual. Baby

Dorothy arrived safely weighing 3 Kg., about
6½ lbs." What unspeakable joy for them and their
family.

How easy it is to identify with the happiness of
proud parents when they tenderly carry their
newborn home. And the joy continues as the child
grows. We goggle with delight when the baby first
attempts to kick or to laugh! The tiny toes, the
knobby knees, the first step and then that exciting
moment when we first hear the word 'Dada' or
'Mama'!

Surely a new baby, with all its potential for
growth, is a miracle beyond human comprehension.
And even more marvelous is a person who has just
been born again—one who has taken the first step
on the journey from spiritual birth to spiritual
maturity.

Unfortunately, however, life does not always
follow the path from the joy of birth to the mature
fulfillment of adulthood. Sadly, the very week we
received the letter announcing the birth of baby
Dorothy, my wife and I also heard that the twenty-
one-year-old daughter of longstanding friends in
Cincinnati, Ohio, had died. Tragically, in her twenty-
one years she had never developed from childhood;
either mentally, physically or socially. Though her
parents lovingly had named her Carol Joy (the song
of joy), when she died Carol was still a baby—a
twenty-one year old baby! Her potential to converse
with her parents had been stunted. From a human

perspective, her life journey had been drastically impaired.

And just as Carol never matured beyond infancy, so, too, many people in the Church today do not seem to have developed beyond spiritual babyhood. Although they may have been Christians for many years, they have never really grown in the Lord. Yet, God has provided spiritual nourishment which, if it is properly digested, will stimulate spiritual growth in the life of every born-again child of God.

The Bible is God's nutrient to prevent your Christian life from being spiritually stunted. If you are to grow from the spiritual curiosity of babyhood, to the spiritual stability of youth and finally to the spiritual maturity of adulthood, it is imperative that you receive daily nutrition from God's Word, the Bible. And reading the Bible is intended by God to be more than merely a matter of duty; it is meant to be a refreshing delight in the life of each hungry Christian who partakes of God's prepared food.

Yes, the Word of God will indeed be a source of constant and growing delight when you understand how to digest it as your own spiritual nourishment.

Through the prophet Isaiah, God graciously invites all those who have a hunger and thirst for spiritual food to dine with Him from His own banqueting table:

> *Ho! Everyone who thirsts, come to the waters; and you who have no money, come, buy and eat . . .*

*Why do you spend money for what is not bread, and your wages for what does not satisfy? Listen diligently to Me, and eat what is good, and let your soul **delight** itself in abundance. **Incline your ear**, and come to Me. **Hear**, and your soul shall live . . . (Isaiah 55:1-3).*

Because many people do not seem to understand how they will receive food for their faith as they read God's Word directly, they find it much easier to read books about the Bible than to actually read the Bible itself. This book in your hands is not intended to explain the Bible, but instead it is meant to encourage you to read the Bible in such a way that it will explain itself! As a result you will increasingly enjoy a life of transparent and intimate fellowship with your Heavenly Father.

I have often said to people who are just beginning to read the Bible as food for their faith:

Read what you understand and soon you may come to something you do not understand. Keep on reading. Before long, you will come to something you *do* understand. Gradually, what you understand will help you to understand what you did not understand!

Does that make sense to you? In other words, never give up.

All over the world—in classrooms, in lecture halls and in libraries—people are digesting academic information that provides them with much 'food for thought'. If we, in like manner, approach the Bible merely as a religious textbook, all we will receive is just that—**food for thought**. Yet the Bible itself warns us that: *Knowledge puffs up*, [but it is] *love* [that] *builds up (1 Corinthians 8:1 NIV)*.

Yes, unless we understand how to properly digest the Word of God, even a knowledge of Bible truth can puff us up with intellectual pride, rather than build us up in our spiritual life. Instead of merely gaining knowledge during our daily time together with our Lord, we need to receive nourishment from His banqueting table that will provide us with '**food for faith**'.

In striking contrast to those who read the Bible as only an academic exercise are the many joyful believers who have discovered the secret of reading the Word of God so that it becomes a practical and living source of true spiritual nourishment in their lives. These Christians are experiencing the growing reality of a life of fellowship with God and in the process are discovering the way of genuine worship and fruitful service. To such people the bondage of self-consciousness will give way to the blessing of God-consciousness.

To approach God confidently and personally each day with an open Bible and an open heart is the wonderful privilege of every born-again Child of God.

The question you may be asking is: What is the best way to read the Bible so that it will nourish my soul and enable me to grow in the love and knowledge of our Lord Jesus Christ? The secret is found in what we will call a *Together Time*—a time for togetherness with the Lord.

Together Time is really a two-way conversation with our living Lord. Through His Word, the Bible, God speaks to His children. As we respond correctly and personally to what God is saying, we will learn how to pray biblically and with expectant faith.

When I speak about 'praying biblically', I mean that we actually use the very words of the Scriptures we are reading when we respond to our Lord in prayer. To pray biblically is to enjoy a growing assurance of praying in accordance with the will of God.

As the Holy Spirit makes God's Word living to us, we use those exact words of Scripture and relate them to the concerns that may be upon our heart. Praying in this way, we will be saved from stereotyped prayers. Instead, when we pray biblically, we will enjoy privileged fellowship with the Lord as we enter into a growing understanding of His own concerns and purposes in our life.

True prayer is not the bending of God's will to mine, but it is the bending of my will to the will of

God. After Joshua had miraculously led the Children of Israel through the River Jordan during the springtime floods, he encountered an unknown 'man'. Joshua knew that in Canaan his mandate from God was to conquer the land and to cleanse it from its pagan practices. Therefore, Joshua asked of this stranger, who had a sword drawn in his hand, *Are you for us or for our adversaries?* The strange answer Joshua received was 'No!' or as the NIV Bible translates the word *Neither*. Joshua assumed from this answer that the stranger would not take sides. Then came the words that clarified the answer given by the stranger: *but as Commander of the army of the Lord I have now come.*

At that point, Joshua rightfully recognized that instead of taking sides, the stranger was about to take control! Falling on his face as an indication of yieldedness, Joshua knew he was in the presence of the *Commander of the Lord's army. For the place where you stand is holy (Joshua 5:13-15).*

Likewise, in our own times of prayer, we should not bring our personal agenda to God and then ask Him to be with us, but instead we should bow in His Holy Presence to attune ourselves to His plans, His purposes and His power.

Thus, to pray biblically is to pray in harmony with the purposes and will of God. And this bending of our will to His can be the growing experience of each one of us as we learn to align ourselves with

God's Word whenever we pray.

Yes, when you prayerfully read the Bible with a genuine desire to hear from God, you will *grow in the grace and knowledge of our Lord and Savior Jesus Christ (2 Peter 3:18)*.

As we have already observed, Isaiah stated that when we incline our ears to really hear God's voice, then we will truly delight in what He has to say.

Spiritual Check-up

1. How long is it since I first became a born-again Christian?
2. Did I ever enjoy a closer fellowship with God than I do now?
3. In comparing my life today with that of five years ago:

   Do I spend more time alone with God?

   Can I better distinguish God's guidance from my own desires?

*Lord, teach me to listen. The
times are noisy and my ears are
weary with the thousand raucous
sounds which continuously
assault them. Give me the spirit
of the boy Samuel when he said to
Thee, "Speak, for thy servant
heareth." Let me hear Thee
speaking in my heart. Let me get
used to the sound of Thy Voice,
that its tones may be familiar
when the sounds of earth die
away and the only sound will be
the music of Thy speaking Voice.
Amen.*

A.W. Tozer

CHAPTER 2

The Head and the Heart

S everal years ago, in the northern part of Kenya, my wife Dorothy and I, had the privilege of teaching the Word of God to a gathering of national pastors and their wives. In order to arrive by 7:00 p.m., in time for the evening meeting, some of these pastors had set out at four o'clock that morning. Motivated strictly by their fervent desire to learn more of the Bible, they had walked that long, wearisome journey under the brutal equatorial sun that had so devastated their land through drought and famine.

It came as a shock for us to find that between sixty and seventy percent of those national pastors did not possess a Bible. Even though many of these dedicated leaders had only been converted as recently as the past two or three years, their glowing testimonies among their own people had been used by God to bring to life many little churches in the African bush.

At the start of our conference, we were able to put a Bible into the hands of each of these pastors. I then proceeded with several days of instruction. My theme was this: "Now that you have a Bible in your **hand**, it will be of no blessing to you until it gets from your hand into your **head**! But even that will not bring you the full blessing that God intends for you in these days. Only when the Bible begins to live as God's Word in your **heart** will this conference have become a lasting blessing to you. It is imperative that you learn how to get the Bible from your hand to your head and then from your head to your heart."

Recently I saw the house in England where I lived when I was converted to Christ in my late teens. Not far from our home was a lamppost under which a fourteen-year old lad, Bob Flint, also received Christ. Bob's conversion dramatically changed his entire life. Because he had already left school and had been working as a laborer on a construction site, at that time in his life young Bob certainly was no scholar!

Yet soon after Bob became a Christian, I was able to persuade him to read his Bible before he went to work each day. Even though he had had absolutely no church background, Bob soon learned how to nourish his spiritual life by personally interacting with the Word of God in a daily *Together Time*.

The Head and the Heart

It was little wonder then that at the age of seventeen, Bob, having enrolled in a Bible correspondence course, received top grades in his study of the book of Daniel! How thrilled I was later to hear that when he joined the military at age eighteen, he continued in his zeal for the Lord. In fact, during his first eight weeks at 'boot camp', he personally prayed with each one of the other seventeen soldiers in his barracks as they in turn reached out to Christ. And then, when he concluded his military service, Bob felt called to begin missionary training. As he was flying his last mission in Germany, however, his military plane crashed, and Bob was called home to be with his Lord.

Near the site of the plane crash, gospel tracts from Bob's backpack were scattered over the German countryside! Indeed, the Word of God had advanced from Bob's hands to his head, and then from his head to his heart, and finally from his heart to the hearts of others. And when Bob died he was merely called out of a living, earth-confined relationship with his Lord into a more wonderful fellowship in the presence of God!

Many people, like Bob, have ready access to formal Bible study resources and training which can encourage them in their Christian walk. And unlike those eager African pastors, most of us do not have to walk for fifteen hours under the equatorial sun to hear the Word of God taught. But whatever our circumstances may be, we should all know how to transform—yes, **transform**—Bible knowledge into heart experience.

Personally, I thank the Lord that early in my Christian life He showed me the distinction between formal Bible study and *Together Time*. Though the involvement of both the head and the heart are vital in our approach to the Word of God, it is important to understand that head knowledge without heart commitment will not lead to spiritual growth.

THE HEAD
Bible Study: its purpose and its problems.

Study to show thyself approved unto God, a workman that needeth not to be ashamed, rightly dividing the word of truth (2 Timothy 2:15 KJ). To formally **study** the Bible, and thereby to become acquainted with its contents, is in itself an exciting and necessary investment of time for every Christian. Whenever possible, take full advantage of the services and teachings of a godly pastor or Bible teacher and let available Bible commentaries help you become mentally familiar with the Word of God. Such a backdrop of information will help you greatly when you draw aside for your own private *Together Time*.

After all, pastor-teachers are part of God's gift to His church. A pastor's supreme ministry is to teach believers the content, the context and the circumstances of the various books of the Bible, chapter by chapter and book by book. From that framework, a pastor is to exhort his congregation to a life of godliness, a state of inner contentment and a concern for perishing souls.

I have before me the record of five lectures which were delivered by such a pastor. Several years ago, Pastor William Still presented these lectures at an Inter-Varsity Theological Students' Conference. After more than a forty-five year ministry at a single church in Aberdeen, Scotland, his ministry was still as vibrant and vital as ever. And, without question, his pastoral ministry reached out far beyond that church in Scotland. Even today a small army of converts and many others who have been influenced by his preaching and teaching are serving Christ literally around the world. In his lectures to his Inter-Varsity students Pastor Still said:

> The pastor is called to feed the sheep, even if the sheep do not want to be fed. He is certainly not to become an entertainer of goats. Let goats entertain goats and let them do it in goatland. You will certainly not turn goats into sheep by pandering to their goatishness ... The most fruitful pastoral duty is to help all sorts of odd sheep live together, and show them how to live in the

world among goats without becoming goat-like.

When you have been born again, it is very important that you become part of a church where you can be blessed through such faithful pastoral ministry.

Unfortunately, some of you who are reading this book may not have access to this kind of pastoral instruction. However, even if you are so privileged as to have the help of a faithful pastor-teacher and do have ready access to Bible commentaries, you should always be aware of the ever-present danger of trying to let what you have learned in your head substitute for the spiritual food God desires to give you in your daily *Together Time*.

No, we must realize that neither the Bible knowledge we acquire from a faithful pastor-teacher, nor even the understanding that we gain from our own intellectual study of God's Word, can take the place of the spiritual food which the Holy Spirit will apply to our hearts and lives as we join with Him in that special *Together Time*.

Of course, just as a Bible teacher is no substitute for a personal *Together Time*, so too, having a personal *Together Time* is no excuse for neglecting the opportunities that God gives us to study His Word and for failing to become part of the ministry of a Bible-believing church.

Whatever your circumstances, the following suggestions may help you develop a more rewarding method of formal Bible study.

A long time ago, Myles Coverdale suggested these questions be used to facilitate a helpful **study** of God's Word. This is a paraphrase of what he wrote:

It will greatly help you to understand Scripture, if you note not only what is spoken or written but also:

Of whom is the passage speaking?
To whom is the passage directed?
What specific words does the writer use?
At what time was the passage written?
From where was the passage written?
For what purpose was the passage written?
In what situation was the passage written?

How does the passage fit into what goes before it and what follows it?

When you form the habit of responding naturally to such questions in your formal Bible study (using a marginal reference Bible whenever possible), you will increasingly thrill at the marvelous gems of truth that harmonize throughout the entire Bible. Gradually, you will be fascinated with the unfolding panorama of prophecy contained in God's revelation, some parts of which have already been fulfilled and some of which yet await fulfillment.

You will also be greatly blessed as your eyes are increasingly and wonderfully opened to your eternal God: His purposes in creation; His place in history; His doctrine of salvation; His coming into the world in the person of the Lord Jesus Christ; and His detailed instruction for Christians like you and me, even to this present hour. Such Bible knowledge is truly fascinating and should be diligently pursued by every believer.

THE HEART
Together Time: its correctives and its counsel.

God's desire for each of His own is that we worship Him in *spirit and truth (John 4:24),* with both our **heart** and our **head**—the two joined in a oneness of personal fellowship with Him.

If your formal Bible study leaves you with only an objective knowledge of the Bible, such knowledge will profit you little! In fact, head knowledge without sincere life-application is a great problem with many Christians today.

Sadly, there are those who know a great deal about the Word of God but who do not live in the light of that wonderful knowledge. Instead, they lock away their knowledge of the Bible in the recesses of their minds and foolishly adopt the ways of the world. What a tragedy, for God's Word never conforms to contemporary thought and life patterns.

To approach the Word of God with the mind-set of the world, and then to try to synchronize the Scriptures with the philosophy or psychology of a humanistic culture is to violate every principle of intellectual honesty and moral integrity. The Lord Jesus Christ paid a tremendous price to deliver us out of this present evil world, and the Word of God certainly contradicts the thought patterns of a Christ-rejecting generation.

Because God's Word never conforms to a humanistic culture, when we study the Bible with the supreme desire of becoming what God wants us to be, it will indeed be a revolutionary life-transforming experience! It is this heart involvement not just a head knowledge that God requires of each of His children.

The psalmist did not say, 'Your Word have I hidden in my **head**.' He did say: *Your Word have I hidden in mine **heart**, that I might not sin against Thee (Psalm 119:11).* In his public tirades, even Adolf Hitler at times quoted from the Bible, but this knowledge of certain Bible verses was of no help to him in his own moral choices nor in his eternal destiny.

Obviously, his knowledge had not penetrated his heart.

But, you may ask, "What did David mean when he said that he had hidden God's Word in his heart?" Certainly he was not talking about the hollow muscular organ which pumped blood from his veins into his arteries. Of course nobody can hide God's Word there! When David used the word **heart**, he referred to the very center of his behavioral life-directing inner self. As we read the Bible to hide God's Word in the center of our being, then, by the power of the indwelling Christ, we will constantly enjoy the purifying, enabling and nourishing vitality of God's Word.

When it was my privilege to formally study the Bible and theology as a full-time student, I learned that the accumulation of biblical truth was no substitute for getting alone with God to hear what He had to say to me through His Word. I also discovered that it was easier to sit in judgment on the Word of God than to let the Word of God sit in judgment upon me.

During those college days we used to laugh when we thought of our flippant definition for a classroom lecture. We said: "A lecture is the means whereby material is transferred from the notebook of the professor to the notebook of the student without its going through the head of either!"

Even more tragic than this, is the situation in which Bible teaching goes through the head of the pastor to the heads of the congregation without its stirring the heart of either. You will remember that God clearly says:

But the word which they heard did not profit them, not being mixed with faith in those who heard it (Hebrews 4:2).

Only when we can identify with the testimony of the prophet Jeremiah will the Word of God bring its intended blessing to our lives. Jeremiah said: *His word was in my heart like a burning fire shut up in my bones . . . (Jeremiah 20:9).* In the lives of many believers today such a flaming conviction about God's Word is sorely missing. There is no real link made between the head and the heart—between the Voice of God and the life of the believer. As a result, there is too often very little correlation between what we know and what we do.

When Bible teaching really stirs your heart, it will most certainly change your life! As this happens, you will find yourself becoming much less dependent upon human support systems, such as family counselors and neatly-packaged seminars, for you will have discovered how God has intended for you to personally appropriate the promises that He has made to you in His Word. Then, by the power of the Spirit's indwelling, you will be able to obey the clear commands of the Lord Jesus Christ.

Occasionally after I have preached, a kindly member of the congregation will seek to encourage me by saying, "You certainly gave me something to think about." When I hear that, I know the sermon has not really accomplished the purpose that I had hoped it would! There is a difference between the Word of God being applauded as an intellectual stimulus, and that of its being applied as a life-transforming Truth. Truly, sermons should give people something to **act upon**, not just something to think about!

Similarly, if a *Together Time* does not lead to an active response of faith, and/or obedience, the confession of sin, or to an attitude of worship, it has **not** been a fruitful *Together Time!*

On the other hand, whenever a child of God has his head filled with the knowledge of God's Word and his heart vibrating with the tender movement of the Holy Spirit, he will truly enjoy living fellowship with the Savior. Even today, when I visit Bible colleges as a guest lecturer, I tell my students:

You are not here to study the Bible just to get to know the Bible! You are here to study the Bible to get to know the God of the Bible!

Spiritual immaturity among believers is mute testimony to the impotency of a few slick phrases and neatly-packaged biblical outlines. Anything that you let take the place of the unique experience of individually drawing aside with God and your open Bible will diminish—and possibly even destroy—your intimate and personal fellowship with God.

True fellowship with the Lord can only occur when the Christian encounters the transparent light of God's holy presence. Such light is very revealing and requires the honesty and frankness of open communication between you and your Heavenly Father. If, when you read His Word, your heart responds obediently to His truth, that truth will become nourishment to your soul and you will grow in the knowledge and wisdom of your Lord. The psalmist testified: *In Your light we see light (Psalm 36:9).* The old adage is still very true:

> Light obeyed brings greater light;
> Light disobeyed brings deeper night.

I am sure you have found, as I have, that it is easier to give counsel to someone else than it is to act upon your own counsel. However, the Lord Jesus, who is described by Isaiah as the *Wonderful Counselor (Isaiah 9:6)*, is unique, for He not only gives counsel, but He also becomes the One who enables us to act upon that counsel.

Each morning your *Together Time* can play a vital role in preparing you for what awaits you later in the day. When, through the reading of His Word, God gives you His counsel, you can be assured that the Lord Jesus will also be your indwelling sufficiency and guide for whatever befalls.

Spiritual Check-up

1. Does my heart respond as readily as my head when I read the Bible?
2. When I pray, am I truly having a two-way communication with God?
3. In my spiritual life, do I first seek counsel from man or from God (through His Word)? (Warning: *They did not wait for **His** counsel . . . Psalm 106:13.*)
4. In my Christian service, does my counsel to others come from a heart that is aflame with God's love and a mind that is filled with His Word? (Warning: *They rebelled against Him by **their** counsel . . . Psalm 106:43.*)

Sins Like These

Sins unnumbered I confess;
Of exceeding sinfulness—

Worldly cares at worship time;
Selfish aims in work sublime;
Pride, when God is passing by;
Sloth, when souls in darkness die;

Tasting that the Lord is good,
Pining then for poisonous food;
At the fountain of the skies
Craving creaturely supplies.

Sins like these my heart deceive,
You—who only know them grieve!

O how lightly have I slept
With the daily wrongs unwept,
Woke to holy labors fresh;
With the plague-spot in my flesh;

Still Your comfort does not fail,
Still Your healing touch avails,
See my sorrow Lord for Thee,
O be merciful to me.

Father, pardon through Your Son,
Sins against your Spirit done.

William Maclardie Bunting
(1805–1866) Adapted by R. A. B.

CHAPTER 3

Prayerful Preparation

When I was first converted, I had very little knowledge of the Bible, but I very soon discerned that when I turned to its pages, I was in fact reading **the Word of God**. To this very day, I still rejoice to realize that the Lord Jesus continues to speak to my heart when I read His Word.

Even as a new Christian, I was taught that when I opened my Bible, the Holy Spirit desired to make it living to my heart. So I would often start my *Together Time* by praying a little prayer that I had learned as a chorus:

Spirit of God, my Teacher be,
Revealing the things of Christ to me,
Place in my hand the wonderful key
That shall unclasp and set me free.

Before leaving His disciples to go to His Father in Heaven, the Lord Jesus Christ promised: *When He, the Spirit of Truth, is come, He will guide you into all truth (John*

16:13). Ultimately there is only one Teacher—the Holy Spirit.

If the Holy Spirit is not free to work in our lives, our reading of the Word of God will remain flat and empty.

John Wesley (who was mightily used of God in the eighteenth-century British revival that many historians credit with saving England from revolution) also knew the value of his *Together Time.* He wisely learned a lesson that we might all do well to emulate. Wesley disciplined himself to go to bed early in the evening to make an early rise in the morning possible. Recently, I knelt alone and prayed on the very prayer-stool where Wesley would meet his Lord at 4:00 a.m.! In that very room I was moved when I read the following quotation from his diary: 'I sit down alone . . . Only God is here. In His presence I open, I read His Book. And what I read I teach.'

And in order to encourage born-again believers, the Apostle John assured them of the sufficiency of the Holy Spirit to touch their hearts through God's Word, even when they would not have other people to help them understand the Scriptures. To them he wrote: *But the anointing which you have received from Him abides in you, and you do not need that anyone teach you* [not 'no one' but not a 'self-apppointed teacher']*; but as the same anointing teaches you concerning all things, and is true, and is not a lie, and just as it has taught you,*

you will abide in Him (1 John 2:27). When you consciously rely upon the illumination of the Holy Spirit as you read God's book, He will make its truth living to your heart.

If you really desire to have a rich, fulfilling and regular *Together Time,* seek to find a quiet place and set aside a specific time to open your Bible and commune with God. Though the prospect of such times alone with God will often thrill your heart in joyful anticipation, there will also be days when your family, or your business, or other interests will vie for your attention and make it difficult for you to go aside to be alone with God. Such days will require real discipline if you are to grow in the love and knowledge of the Lord Jesus Christ. Remember, a neglected Bible is just as useless as if you did not have one.

Even as the Israelites had to make daily preparations to gather the manna that God had divinely provided for their physical sustenance on their way to the Promised Land, so, too, we need to ready ourselves to take in the Word of God.

First: It might be helpful for you to actually bend your knees when you open your Bible to be alone with God.

Second: When you come to Him who is Eternal Light, it is always necessary to bare your heart in His Holy Presence. You can hide nothing from Him, so why try?

Once you have prepared yourself for your encounter with God, the Bible will come alive with glowing reality and you will begin to discover how the Word of God will move from your head to your heart.

BEND YOUR KNEES
Living fellowship cannot co-exist with a proud spirit.

In the Bible, we read about many godly people who expressed their reverence and submission to God by assuming the kneeling position. Though liturgical Christians and practicing Muslims make a habit of kneeling in their public prayers, such a posture does not necessarily indicate a living fellowship with God. However, when we do come to our Eternal God and Creator, our attitude of mind and heart can be greatly helped if we kneel before Him.

In the Garden of Gethsemane, when the Lord Jesus Christ was approaching the dreadful hour of His crucifixion, He saw that His disciples were fast asleep. After having withdrawn a distance from them, Jesus *kneeled down, and prayed (Luke 22:41)*. Jesus was alone with His Father. There He **knelt** to pray. Likewise, when we separate ourselves from our friends and our family to be alone with God, we, too, might find it helpful to express our reverence to Him and our commitment to His will by kneeling as we pray.

When the Apostle Paul was nearing the end of his public ministry, he made a point of saying a fond goodbye to the church that he had established at Ephesus. We read how *he knelt down and prayed with them all (Acts 20:36).* On the seashore at another time, Paul said goodbye to the disciples and their wives and children. The Scriptures record that they *knelt down on the shore and prayed (Acts 21:5).* Many today might think that the sight of women and children kneeling to pray in a public place would be misconstrued by bystanders. In a day when we fear being accused of fanaticism, we, too, often opt for casual comfort in a private prayer meeting. Obviously, the disciples, along with the women and the children of Paul's day, had no such problem with kneeling. Neither should we, whether we are in a public prayer meeting or whether we are alone with God.

It must be remembered, however, that, whether we stand, sit or walk when we pray, the important thing about our private communion with God is our attitude of mind. Yes, when we pray, the Bible tells us to adopt the right mental attitude, for: *God resisteth the proud, but giveth grace unto the humble. Submit yourselves therefore to God. Resist the devil, and he will flee from you. Draw near to God, and He will draw nigh to you (James 4:6-8 KJ).*

Because of certain physical problems, it may be impossible for some people to kneel for an extended period of prayer. Happily, God sees each of our hearts. Certainly our heart attitude is more important to Him than is our posture. But for those who are able, kneeling can be a very helpful way of sharpening our understanding of the fact that when we pray we have the awesome privilege of talking to our Creator—as friend with Friend! For each of us, the all-important biblical injunction is: *Humble yourselves in the sight of the Lord*, and as we respond to this command, God continues with a wonderful promise: *and He will lift you up (James 4:10)*.

BARE YOUR HEART
Living fellowship always commences at God's Mercy Seat, which in New Testament terms is at the Cross upon which Jesus died.

Yes, even before the Lord Jesus died on the Cross, in His great mercy and love, God had chosen to accept the death of His innocent Son as a sin payment so that wayward mankind would be able to renew fellowship with Him. So, long before the crucifixion of our Savior, God declared that He would meet with His children at the Mercy Seat: *And there I will meet with thee, and I will commune with thee from above the Mercy Seat (Exodus 25:22 KJ)*.

Today the sacrifice for our sin is part of history; the precious Blood of the Lord Jesus Christ has been shed on our behalf and thus, through Jesus' death, a new and living way has been provided for us to commune with Him. His inconceivable love enables us to joyfully exclaim: *Let us therefore come boldly to the throne of grace, that we may obtain mercy and find grace to help in time of need (Hebrews 4:16)*.

Mercy means that God does not give us what we do deserve; grace means that God does give us what we do not deserve. How wonderful to walk in fellowship with our God of mercy and grace.

From every stormy wind that blows,
From every swelling tide of woes,
There is a calm, a sure retreat;
'Tis found beneath the mercy seat.

There is a place where Jesus sheds
The oil of gladness on our heads,
A place that is to me so sweet;
It is the blood-bought mercy seat.

There is a spot where spirits blend,
Where friend holds fellowship with Friend;
Though sundered far, by faith they meet
Around one common mercy seat.

Ah! whither could we flee for aid,
When tempted, desolate, dismayed;
Or how the host of hell defeat,
Had suffering saints no mercy seat?

There, there, on eagle's wings we soar,
And time and sense seem all no more,
And heaven comes down, our souls to greet,
And glory crowns the mercy seat.

H. Stowell

Living fellowship cannot co-exist with an impure conscience.

A boy that is born into a family will always be the son of his parents. He can never be 'un-born'! But if that child is naughty, there will be times when open communication with his parents will be broken. The relationship remains, but fellowship is certainly severed! That is a great tragedy.

It is wonderful for us to bathe in the knowledge that the moment we were born again, an eternal relationship was established with our Father in heaven. If we sincerely received the Lord Jesus Christ into our hearts, we became the children of God, a relationship that will remain for eternity. However, when we sin, our fellowship with our Father is tragically severed.

Because of our disobedience, we will no longer sense the same blessing of His smile upon our lives that we once enjoyed. And this break in transparent fellowship, whether short-lived or long-lasting, certainly cannot be attributed to God or His lack of concern. The rift is always due to our own defiled conscience; we are the sole cause of any interruption of fellowship with God.

An Impure Conscience: John Bunyan once said: "Sin will keep me from the Bible and the Bible will keep me from sin." When a person has grieved the Holy Spirit and has consciously embraced sin in his life, he will also lose his appetite for the Word of

God. A pure conscience is absolutely essential for the Christian to have a vibrant and expectant faith when he turns to God's Word. The Bible states: *without faith it is impossible to please Him, for he who comes to God must believe that He is, and that he is a rewarder of those who diligently seek Him (Hebrews 11:6).*

But if we persist in ignoring our sin, when we read the Bible our faith will be quenched because our conscience will no longer be attuned to the voice of the Holy Spirit.

A Clean Conscience: To renew fellowship with God after we have sinned, it is necessary that our guilty, sin-laden conscience be cleansed. To rid himself of this burden of guilt, the defiled Christian must bare his heart in confession of his sin before God. The Apostle John wrote:

If we confess our sins, He is faithful and just to forgive us our sins and to cleanse us from all unrighteousness (1 John 1:9).

In that portion of my Bible I have recorded a prayer as it was prayed by F. W. Krummacher. When I become conscious of my own failure and sin, I try to name those specific sins before God's Mercy Seat. Then I will sometimes pray Krummacher's prayer as the basis of my own private confession to the Lord:

O Lord, my God, I have sinned against You afresh and am grieved by it. I judge and condemn myself; but Your mercy is great and therein do I trust. Sprinkle my conscience with the Blood of the atonement, and enable me, by faith, to appropriate for this my sin, the sufferings You have endured for me.

We do not commit our sins in bundles, so why should we try to confess them in one general admission of guilt? Asking God to forgive us for 'all our sins' in one lump sum is more likely to be an attempt to find an easy way out for our proud hearts than to be a sincere expression of repentance and the desire to step back into the will of God. This type of all-encompassing confession does little to really clear the conscience of its guilt. When the Holy Spirit brings to mind anything that is known to be sin, we must name that act of disobedience with the very word that the Bible uses to describe such a sin—not a white lie, but a lie; not a mind that fantasizes, but an adulterous mind; not a hasty word, but a heart filled with murderous hate.

Because real guilt, and not just a guilt complex, is our problem, there should never be any psychological double talk or human excuse when we come into the light of God's presence. When, humbly and honestly, you name your sin before Him, God, in His great mercy, will respond to your confession. Such is the wonderful grace of God.

After David had confessed his own tragic sin, he rejoiced to reflect upon: *the multitude of Your* [God's] *tender mercies (Psalm 51:1)*. The Bible record in

Psalm 51 shows that when David turned to God, this broken and heart-stirred man was not only honest in his confession, but he was also genuine in his repentance. If you repent (recognize that you have taken your own path rather than God's and now desire to return to God's pure and holy way) and then make humble and honest confession of your conscious sins and name them in specific terms before God, you, too, will rejoice in the multitude of God's tender mercies. Only then will your conscience be clean so that you will once again be able to resume fellowship with a Holy God.

And when your conscience has been cleansed by the merciful act of a loving God, you will find that you have a new boldness in prayer.

Therefore, brethren, having boldness to enter the Holiest by the blood of Jesus . . . let us draw near with a true heart in full assurance of faith, having our hearts sprinkled from an evil conscience . . . (Hebrews 10:19,22).

Yes, true boldness before God flows from a clean conscience. Then a transparently truthful heart will release the type of bold faith which is a virtual prerequisite to the full enjoyment of living fellowship with God.

When you know your heart is clean, the humbling memory of past sin will no longer be able to disturb your conscience. Of course, Satan will try to accuse you, but to thwart his strongest attacks, your answer to him must be the same as God's answer to your guilty conscience; that is, the power of the precious Blood of Jesus. In the book of Revelation, saints, who were being accused by Satan of the very sins that God had forgiven, understood the mighty power of that precious Blood. Of them it is recorded: *And they overcame him* [Satan—the accuser of the brethren] **by the blood of the Lamb** . . . *(Revelation 12:11)*. Not only did they enjoy the blessing of a cleansed conscience, but they had also learned the secret of an undisturbed conscience. Hallelujah!

Living fellowship cannot co-exist with a wrong mind-set.

There is often a hidden reason why people do not have a desire for the nourishing milk of God's Word. Have you ever had such a fever that you lost your appetite? No matter how tasty the food might have been, you were not interested in eating. Likewise, just as a nourishing meal may not be attractive to you when you are ill, the Bible will hold no fascination if a wrong mind-set has quenched your spiritual appetite.

Though Peter encourages us to desire the nourishing *milk of the Word (1 Peter 2:2)*, he first warns us of those attitudes that will destroy our desire for God's nutrition. Bluntly, he also records that there is only one way to deal with these hindrances to a nourishing *Together Time*. Every hindrance to a wholesome spiritual appetite must be laid aside. The unhealthy mind-set has to be radically changed if a healthy appetite is to be restored—this is another way of saying 'repent'!

> *Therefore, laying aside all **malice**, all **guile**, **hypocrisy**, **envy**, and all **evil speaking** . . . desire the pure milk of the word, that you may grow thereby (1 Peter 2:1-2).*

Scripture emphatically states that we will never really desire 'the pure milk of the Word' until the before-mentioned spiritual sicknesses—which ruin our spiritual appetite—have been dealt with. Let us consider them one at a time:

Malice: Our resentment or anger for the way we have been treated by others—having an unforgiving spirit.

Corrie Ten Boom endured incredible suffering in the notorious extermination center at the Ravensbruck Nazi concentration camp. Even more horrific for her was to witness her own beloved and saintly sister's life ebb away in the inhumane and torturous circumstances of that camp. Speaking of the cruel guards who had been responsible for such atrocities, Corrie Ten Boom later testified how she had truly forgiven them and said:

"Forgiveness is an act of the will; and the will can choose to act regardless of the temperature of the heart."

If you harbor an unforgiving spirit to anyone—no matter how you may have suffered at such a person's hands—your lack of forgiveness will not harm them, but it will certainly throttle your spiritual life! In fact, you will be in bondage to such a person until you have willed to forgive them. Only then can you pray the prayer our Lord taught us to pray: *forgive us our sins, for we also forgive everyone who is indebted to us (Luke 11:4)*. If you are aware of a spirit of 'malice' (unforgiveness) in your heart, choose to forgive that person, or persons, as you spend time alone with God. Then you will be able to express God's love towards them without hypocrisy!

Guile: Our covering up or rationalizing our failure rather than confessing our sin—living an existence of deceit rather than of honesty.

Hypocrisy: Overt misrepresentation of ourselves in a proud desire to give a wrong impression—pretending to be someone or something we are not. A desire for approval—whether from a pastor, a parent, a friend, or at the workplace—is at the root of all hypocrisy.

Envy: The reacting to another's blessings with suspicion rather than with genuine rejoicing—coveting what somebody else possesses.

Evil Speaking: The use of our tongue to hurt or malign another, or the lending of our ear to anything that would defame another's character—trying to ease our own personal guilt by pointing to the sins in the life of another person.

These are the things that we must lay aside if we truly desire to be nourished by the Word. Then, just as a newborn baby does not need persuasion to seek life-giving milk when nursing time comes around, so, too, when you have an opportunity to open your Bible, you will *desire the pure milk of the word, that you may grow thereby (1 Peter 2:2).*

Living fellowship cannot co-exist with a self-centered life.

Recently I was privy to a letter from a lady missionary who has been in Japan for many years. She ministers to people most others cannot reach—those in government and diplomatic circles and others in 'high-society'. She wrote:

Whatever happened to the teaching of denying self and taking up the cross daily? As I sorted books relating to the Christian life, something came to my attention. Many of the themes of the books I have acquired in the past twenty or so years boiled down to 'do it yourself' improvements for the Christian life. But I remember that the books from my early Christian life were about denying self, daily taking up the cross, living a holy life, abiding in Christ and allowing Him to live through me. Are those teachings gradually disappearing or am I imagining it?

Maybe that is what a Chinese leader in Hong Kong meant when he wrote: "In the West, or in the free world as a whole, I see the church identifying far more with the powerful victory of Jesus' resurrection. They want that kind of relationship. They are keen for the success, the prosperity, the good things of the risen Son. Few partake in the fellowship of Christ's sufferings. However, I see the opposite in the Asian Church, particularly in countries where situations are confining and restrictive. These believers are more willing to fellowship with the sufferings of Christ. For them, *the fellowship of His sufferings* is their greater reward and privilege."

Conformed to His Death
The Apostle Paul himself prayed:

That I may know Him [the Lord Jesus], *and the power of His resurrection, and the fellowship of His sufferings, being conformed to His death (Philippians 3:10).*

Amos helps us to grasp the implications of this noble ambition to fellowship with the Lord Jesus as expressed by Paul when he asked: *Can two walk together, unless they be agreed? (Amos 3:3)*. If we desire to walk in the power of His resurrection, then we should also surely agree to share in the fellowship of His sufferings. Half an agreement is really no agreement at all!

Elsewhere Paul pinpointed the great pain of unrequited love when he wrote to his own converts who had begun to despise his apostolic authority: *I will very gladly spend and be spent for your souls; though the more abundantly I love you, the less I am loved (2 Corinthians 12:15)*. Elsewhere he analyzed genuine love and emphatically declared: *love suffers long and . . . does not seek its own . . . (1 Corinthians 13:4-5)*.

Such pure love, that was both long-suffering and unselfish, was wonderfully personified in the person of the Lord Jesus Christ. When the Lord Jesus came into a loveless world, He perfectly demonstrated the love of God in human form. His deeds, His words, His innermost thoughts, His all-consuming commitment to His Father's will—all painted an exquisite picture of love that was never self-serving. In other words, from the moment He was cradled to the moment He was crucified, the Lord Jesus lovingly refused to exercise the overwhelming advantages of His own human perfection to seek His own personal benefits.

Accordingly, during His thirty-three years on earth, the Lord Jesus continually *laid down His life (1 John 3:16)* for the good of other people. Then as He faced the agony of the Cross, we read:

Jesus knew that His hour had come that He should depart from this world to the Father, having loved his own who were in the world, He loved them to the end (John 13:1).

Yes, His love certainly **suffered long**. So, if we would truly 'fellowship' with our Savior, the heartsearching question we must now ask ourselves is:

Do I use the advantages of life that God has given me for my own benefit and advancement; or am I prepared to lay down *my* life in genuine love for other people even if it does involve suffering in the process?

Yes, God's love portrays a stark contrast to our current 'me-first' generation, which boldly declares that self-love is a virtue and that one's rights are more important than the welfare of others. It is this very worshiping of self that the Scriptures reveal as one of the signs of the last days: *men shall be lovers of their own selves . . . lovers of pleasure more than lovers of God (2 Timothy 3:2,4 KJ).*

It is not surprising, then, that Alexander Maclaren insisted that the pathway to loftier spiritual beauties is stained with the bloodied footprints of wounded self-love.

Sin, whether expressed by deed or in thought, bears evidence of our inherited disposition of self-consciousness and self-centeredness. Oswald

Chambers defines this selfish bias as "my claim to my right to myself," and declares that it is "equally dangerous whether it is worked out in respectable morality or whether it is worked out in vile immorality." It is easy to deplore the selfishness and ruthlessness of theft and exploitation, but we need also to realize that man's sinful self-centeredness is likewise expressed in more subtle ways.

Not surprisingly, at the heart of every domestic problem and social tension, and even at the heart of most church difficulties, is the insidious claim of my right to myself—my time, my money, my way, my desire, my will. Indeed, anything that does not reflect the love of God, which seeks not its own, is an expression of man's inherent selfishness.

MY HEAVENLY PERSPECTIVE

The only way we can truly recognize self-centeredness is to look at ourselves from God's point of view. J. B. Phillips in his *Letters to Young Churches* transliterates Paul's prayer for the people in the church at Colossae like this:

*We are asking God that you may see things from **His point of view** by being given spiritual insight and understanding (Colossians 1:9).*

Only when we follow Paul's example and pray for God to open our spiritual eyes will we begin to view the 'true' circumstances of our personal life, not through the eyes of our self-centered existence, but from God's heavenly perspective. And only in this way can we look at the realities of our life through His spiritual prism.

One night Mrs. Silence, a long time friend of Dorothy's and mine, was greatly comforted when she prayerfully and obediently faced a family crisis from a heavenly perspective. She was awakened at 2:00 a.m. by a telephone call. "Do you know who was driving your car tonight?" asked a police officer. "Yes, my two sons are driving home from a young people's Bible Conference," she apprehensively replied. "Well, I have sad news for you—the driver fell asleep and your car is wrapped around a tree on the side of the road. The driver of the car is dead and there is virtually no hope that the other young man will live!" This shocking news stunned the bewildered mother, whose heart had always been filled with tender love for her children.

Putting down the telephone, Mrs. Silence cried to her Heavenly Father, "O God, what does a mother do at a time like this?" Fortunately, she had learned to pray and think biblically. She told me later that all she could reflect upon was the verse of Scripture that commanded, *In everything give thanks (1 Thessalonians 5:18).* "But Lord," Mrs. Silence continued, "You know my heart is not thankful. It is cold and shocked and empty, but on this terrible night I will obey Your Word. As I do, please perform a miracle in my heart. When I obey You and say thank You, You will have to make it real because, in this tragic hour, I do not feel at all thankful." In this way, Mrs. Silence exercised her faith and began to pray.

This tender-hearted mother told me that when she first said, "Thank You, Father, for who You are," her stunned heart remained both cold and empty. But as she faithfully repeated her thanks, the Holy Spirit performed His own wonderful miracle! He filled her heart with comfort and genuine thanksgiving. Yes, during those long dark hours of night, God's Comforter, the Holy Spirit, responded to the faith and obedience of Mrs. Silence. He reassured her of God's unchanging love to both her and her family. As the morning dawned, no doubt, there were still tears in her eyes, but at the same time she experienced the indescribable comfort of God's peace ruling in her heart.

This is a wonderful testimony of the grace of God as He enfolded a grieving mother to His bosom of eternal love. With deep and quiet confidence, Mrs. Silence said how during that dark night the peace of God, which passes human understanding, had flooded her soul. As Mrs. Silence proved in her walk with the Lord, when trouble comes, there is a total difference between a human and a heavenly viewpoint.

As you too enjoy an intimate fellowship with God you will come to realize that thanksgiving and faith are always interrelated. When the thanksgiving of genuine faith fills your heart, God will enable you to

view the changing circumstances of your life—
whether they outwardly appear good or bad—from
His point of view. From such a heavenly perspective,
God will certainly reassure your hurting heart that
All things **really do** *work together for good to those who
love God, to those who are the called according to His
purpose (Romans 8:28).* The comfort of this verse need
not remain a cold, empty, oft-quoted truth. God has
given us this wonderful promise that it may ring with
miraculous reality in each of our hearts. So praise
the Lord when you feel like it! Praise the Lord when
you don't feel like it! And keep on praising the Lord
until you do feel like it! There will never be a
circumstance in your life or mine when it is
inopportune for us to praise the Lord.

Recently, Dorothy and I received a letter from
long-term missionaries who have faithfully and
fruitfully ministered for Christ in the restrictive
circumstances of a Middle East country. In his letter
Stan wrote: "I can and must praise the Lord on the
basis of His character—not my comfort." To amplify
Corrie Ten Boom's statement about forgiveness, we
could also say that since praising the Lord is an act of
the will, the will can choose to praise the Lord
regardless of the temperature of the heart! Then as
we choose to praise Him, He will surely give us the
inner glow of His peace and the abiding assurance of
His unchanging love—no matter what our
circumstance may be.

Notice we are not told to give thanks to God **for**
everything; but to give Him thanks **in** everything.

Genuine thanksgiving, which flows from a recognition of our heavenly perspective, is the one ingredient of faith that separates self-pity from grief.

Remember, this is true whether we are in a church or in a hospital! Even when the storms of life assail, though an earthbound heart will find it easier to reflect a 'pity me' attitude, a Christ-centered heart will still praise the Lord.

Most of us fall and collapse at the first grip of pain; we sit down on the threshold of God's purposes and wilt with self-pity. Even so-called Christian sympathy will only accelerate the process. But, in His great love, God will never do that. He comes with the grip of the pierced hand of His Son, and says—"Enter into fellowship with me; arise and shine." If through a broken heart God can bring His purpose to pass in the world, then thank Him for breaking your heart (Oswald Chambers, *My Utmost for His Highest*, paraphrase).

Notice God's loving reason behind the *"all things"* in our lives. The very next verse reveals that they are purposed so that we *"be conformed to the image of His Son" (Romans 8:29).*

Yes, if we are to understand how God has provided us with a glorious freedom from ourselves, it is essential that we learn to view our life from a heavenly perspective.

God's answer to a self-centered life is not improvement nor education, **but death!** When we are confronted with the gravitational pull of the self-life during our lives on earth, genuine faith will be able to rejoice in God's eternal truth: *For you died, and your life is hidden with Christ in God (Colossians 3:3).*

Because we are *hidden with Christ in God*—through the process of **death, burial and resurrection** *(Romans 6:2-4)*—we have already been radically severed from our earthbound existence with its self-centered concerns. Now we can enjoy our new perspective of life on the resurrection side of the Cross!

> In Christ I died, in Christ I rose,
> In Christ I triumphed o'er my foes,
> In Christ in Heaven I took my seat,
> And Heaven rejoiced at hell's defeat.

Dead to the old creation, the true Christian has become part of God's new creation. That is what our salvation is all about.

As we understand our positional co-crucifixion with Christ, our daily life on earth will be transformed from that of being a self-centered existence to that of being a Christ-centered experience. But to constantly enjoy such intimate fellowship with Him we must know how to constantly deal with the self life—our earthly problem!

MY EARTHLY PROBLEM

Now we should ask the heart-searching question: "Is my life on earth really Christ-centered or is it still self-centered?"

Certainly, a self-centered life will quickly become hostile to any person or angry at any circumstance that threatens its security, its ego, its comfort or its pleasure. G. Campbell Morgan put it this way: "Self-centeredness is the essence of sin; the core of hostility; the substance out of which hell is made" (*Hosea: The Heart and Holiness of God*).

One evening in a prayer meeting, I heard a lady pray with unusual sincerity. She was obviously meeting God in a new and life-transforming way as she prayed: "Lord Jesus, throw Your arms of love around me, fold me to the cross and love me to death. I want it to be no longer I who lives but Christ who lives in me!" Her prayer impressed me greatly.

Though this lady knew that she had already been delivered—through the process of death and resurrection—to dwell in the heavenlies with Christ, she was also conscious that her body was still very much in this world! Evidently, as she prayed, she was seeking God's solution to the selfish deeds and words of her body here on earth. Such a meaningful prayer surely expressed her fervent desire for a more intimate fellowship with her Lord. As I later reflected upon this prayer, I realized that Paul had given the biblical basis for such a heart-agonizing petition when he wrote: *For if you live according to the flesh you will die;*

but if by the Spirit you put to death the deeds of the body, you will live (Romans 8:13).

Some of my readers may find the next thoughts helpful as an in-depth meditation upon the significance of this verse, while others may find the illustration of the subsequent paragraph to be more helpful and practical. Those who are familiar with the Greek language give us an even fuller understanding of the liberating truth found in this verse:

For if you live according to the flesh you will die; but if by the Spirit you put to death the deeds of the body, you will live (Romans 8:13).

First: In the original Greek the word **you** is the subject of the phrase **put to death** and it is written in the **active voice**.

Biblical fact: If I am to be delivered from the 'deeds' of my body (my self-centered life) I must actively and positively co-operate with God.

Second: This verse also tells us that it is **through the Spirit** (God's Divine Executioner) that He makes His own wonderful provision for victory over our selfish, earthbound deeds.

Biblical fact: Though I must be prayerfully and actively involved in the process, by myself I cannot bring to death my selfish deeds! While I am in this world, **it is only the Holy Spirit who can radically sever me from my self-centered acts**.

Third: It is also interesting to observe that this verse is written in the **present tense**. In practical terms, the use of this tense indicates that my prayerful and active co-operation with God must be **continually** exercised.

Biblical fact: Though it can be a transforming experience the first time a Christian asks the Holy Spirit to love his self-life to death, it is not something that is to be done only once. No, whenever the self-life rears its ugly head there must be specific prayer on our part to co-operate with the liberating work of the Holy Spirit. Then, as we constantly rely on the executing ministry of the Holy Spirit our selfish deeds will indeed be brought to death.

God intends that, on our part, this attitude of faith should be a continual, ongoing, everpresent experience!

To illustrate this, let us go in our imagination to a courtroom. There a man is being tried for murder. The evidence has been sifted, the man's guilt has been established, and now the judge has the solemn responsibility of pronouncing sentence. A hush falls over the courtroom as the judge rises and says: "This man has been found guilty of murder and is therefore condemned to die."

With that somber statement the task of the judge has been completed. If, however, the judge were to try to carry out the sentence of death himself by taking a pistol from under his bench and shooting the murderer, the judge himself would become guilty of murder!

After having announced the sentence of death, all the judge can do is hand the condemned man over to the State executioner.

In the same way, our self-life can do nothing but recognize and confess its selfishness. Like the judge in the courtroom, we must pronounce the judgment of death upon all our selfish deeds. But just as the judge could never take the life of the murderer, so, too, we in our self-centered condition do not have the power to put to death the deeds of the self-life. But, thank God, He has provided a Divine Executioner—the Holy Spirit—and it is the Holy Spirit who has the power to render inoperative the potential selfishness of our lives.

Yes, by God's grace, it is 'through the Spirit' that we are enabled to bring to death the 'deeds of the body'. As we avail ourselves of this wonderful provision on a continual and deliberate basis, we will come to experience the liberating joy of a life that is truly Christ-centered.

Because of such clear Scriptural teaching, and the moving lessons of such earnest prayers as I heard from the lips of the lady in the prayer meeting, I too, have many times prayed in a similar vein:

Lord, by Your Holy Spirit, enfold me to the Cross and love my self-life to death. I want it to be no longer I who live but: Christ who lives in me!

It is easy to think that the ultimate purpose for our being nourished and nurtured with the Word of God is that we may graduate to a life of personal contentment. Not so! Why did the Old Testament priest nurture and nourish the very best of his flock? Merely to have the finest specimens to put on display? On the contrary, as William Still points out, they were the very sheep that were needed for the slaughter! They were purposed from their birth to be a sacrifice!

Too often, Christians wrongly conclude that their musical or oratorical abilities will somehow please Christ as they attempt to become the gold medalist before a crowd of evangelical spectators! When God, with loving provision, nourishes us from His Word, His purpose is not that we may make a better platform appearance, but that every area of our lives be laid out on His altar of sacrifice. Before we can be alive to all that He is, there must first be death to all that we are in ourselves—our self-pity, our self-sufficiency, our self-centeredness, our self-pleasing, our self-vindication . . . the list goes on and on.[*]

With a pained heart the Apostle Paul stated that, apart from Timothy, he could find no other person who would 'care' for the church at Colossae. Because

---

[*] In the Bible, death never means extinction but separation. For instance, physical death is the separation of the soul from the body and eternal death is the eternal separation of the soul from God. In a similar meaning, death to the self-life is the continual separation of selfish deeds from human behavior patterns. And this, as we have seen, can only be accomplished in the power of God's Holy Spirit.

many Christians in that city did not know through their own experience that love *'seeks not its own,'* we read how Paul sadly reflected: *For all seek their own, not the things which are of Christ Jesus (Philippians 2:21).*

Where are the Christians today who **really** care about the suffering church in so many parts of the world? Are we so preoccupied with life as it affects us that we have no time to love people who have nobody else to really care for them? And we must remember that it is only God's love that seeks not its own and suffers long. And, just as a cup full of vinegar must first be emptied of its bitterness before it can be the receptacle of sweet, luscious orange juice, so our self-life must first be brought to death before we can be filled with the love of God. Praise God that both of these ministries are part of the Holy Spirit's gracious work in our lives. How needful it is for all of us to continually ask the Holy Spirit to bring to death by radical separation the deeds of the self-life and, in turn, to fill us to overflowing with the love of God: *Because the love of God has been poured out in our hearts by the Holy Spirit who was given to us (Romans 5:5).*

As these truths begin to vibrate in your heart during your *Together Time*, the Holy Spirit will open fresh truth to you from the Word of God.

It has well been said that every believer should 'keep short accounts with God.' Let us constantly make sure there is nothing in life that will stifle our God-consciousness and intimate fellowship with Him.

Spiritual Check-up

1. In the presence of my Lord, am I aware of any unconfessed sin of which I have not repented?
2. Do I have a problem with:
   An unforgiving spirit?
   Loving people I do not like?
   Deceiving people to project a good image?
   Coveting another person's gifts or possessions?
   Murmuring and criticism?
3. Can I exercise an expectant faith because my conscience has been cleansed?
4. Is my life on earth really Christ-centered or is it still self-centered?

Now, you may want to turn again to the prayer of William Maclardie Bunting (page 46) and then quietly and thoughtfully pray it again yourself.

When we walk with the Lord
In the light of His Word,
What a glory he sheds on our way!
While we do His good will,
He abides with us still
And with all who will trust and obey.

Not a shadow can rise,
Not a cloud in the skies,
But his smile quickly drives it away;
Not a doubt nor a fear,
Not a sigh nor a tear
Can abide while we trust and obey.

But we never can prove
The delights of His love
Until all on the altar we lay;
For the favor He shows
And the joy he bestows
Are for them who will trust and obey.

Then in fellowship sweet
We shall sit at His feet,
Or we'll walk by His side in the way;
What He says we will do,
Where He sends we will will go—
Never fear, only trust and obey.

John H. Sammis

CHAPTER 4

Together Time

When you think of it, there are few greater expressions of pride than that of thinking that we are adequate to meet the challenges of the day, without first drawing upon the sufficiency of the Lord Jesus Christ with an open Bible and an open heart.

David identified the germinal seed that will develop a spiritually productive life. He said the person who meditates upon the Word of God is the person who will, bring forth fruit in season . . . *and whatsoever he doeth shall prosper (Psalm 1:3 KJ).*

What kind of person does God promise to prosper? It is one whose *delight is in the law of the Lord; and in His law doth he meditate day and night* (Psalm 1:2 KJ).

I sometimes say to people who have just received the Lord Jesus into their hearts and lives: "A chapter a day keeps the devil at bay!" Read your portion of Scripture and then return to read it again. As you do, you will be able to **meditate** upon it verse by verse. Have you ever seen a cow in a field chewing her cud? The grass is chewed, swallowed and then brought back into the cow's mouth to be chewed again until all the nourishment has been extracted. This is a good illustration of what true meditation upon the Word of God is all about!

I knew a man who was converted on his seventieth birthday. At that time, he knew very little of the Bible. Before he found new life in Christ, he was not even a church-goer; neither did his skills include academic pursuits. However, after his new-birth experience, such was his desire to grow in grace and in the love and knowledge of the Lord Jesus Christ, that by the time he went to Heaven at age eighty-three, he had read the Bible from cover to cover thirteen times. Whatever your age or educational background you too, can read the Bible each day.

An open Bible, a clean heart, a humble spirit and the prayer of David: *Open my eyes, that I may see wondrous things from Your law (Psalm 119:18),* will prepare the way for a fruitful time with the Lord.

As we have already noted, some people do not realize that a *Together Time* is really a two-way conversation. God speaks to us when we meditate upon the Bible verses we are reading. Unfortunately, many people fail to understand that after God has lovingly condescended to speak to our hearts, He then waits for us to respond to Him in prayer. When we **reflect** upon the Word of God, that Word becomes part of our **thinking**. When we prayerfully **act** upon the Word of God, it becomes part of our **living**.

At this point you may be asking, "How will God speak to me when I read the Bible?" Personally, I have found it helpful to reflect on each verse I read with certain questions in my mind. Some of them were suggested to me many years ago. I let these questions guide me as I prayerfully commune with my Lord. Let me suggest that you, too, guide your thinking in such a fashion as you meditate upon God's Word. Because I have depended upon these questions for so many years, they have become second nature to me when I draw aside to be with God and the Scriptures.

You will notice that some of the following questions will require an act of obedience; others will necessitate a response of faith; still others will result in your being drawn out in worship and praise before the Lord; and finally some will help you discern the subtle devices of your enemy, the devil, and also enable you to understand how Christ's victory over Satan can become yours.

An Act of Obedience

We have already understood that we must keep short accounts with God if we are to be finely tuned to the voice of the Holy Spirit when we read the Bible. But, each time the Holy Spirit does speak to our heart it is also necessary to obey what He is saying.

When reading the Bible in your time together with the Lord, it is good to ask: Is there in this verse—

> A command to obey?
> A sin to avoid?
> A good example to follow?
> A bad example to avoid?

Do you see how such questions can draw you into a personal, two-way relationship with your Lord? They will certainly not leave you merely thinking about the truth you have read. When you answer these questions in the presence of God, you will find it necessary to actively respond in your heart to what God has said.

Always remember that the Holy Spirit Himself is with you when you read God's Word, and, if you rely upon Him, He will push the Word of God nine inches lower—from your head to your heart!

We all live in perilous days as the world races forward in rebellion, and in disobedience to God's commands. To influence a Christ-rejecting generation, we must be obedient and whole-hearted. Only when we begin to **obey** the truths that God shows us will we be open for His power to flow through us to a needy world.

Recently, my wife and I shared a reading from Oswald Chambers' book *My Utmost for His Highest*. This is a paraphrase of what we read:

> Obey God in the thing He shows you, and instantly the next thing is opened up . . . "I suppose I will understand that some day!" you say. But just a minute; you can understand it right now! **It is not study** that brings special insight; **it is obedience**. Even the tiniest fragment of obedience will open the windows of heaven so that the most profound truths of God will be there for you right away. But God will never reveal additional truth about Himself until you have obeyed what you already know.

It is reported that one night two great missionary pioneers, Charles T. Studd and Hudson Taylor, shared an attic room. Early in the morning, Taylor awakened to find his roommate poring over an open Bible as it was illuminated by a flickering candle and asked how long he had been there. In answer to Taylor's question, Studd confessed:

"At midnight, I awoke with the words of the Lord Jesus on my mind: *If you love Me, keep My commandments (John 14:15)*. I asked myself if I had proved my love to the Lord Jesus by total obedience? Reaching for my Bible, I spent the rest of the night reading the gospels. There I searched for every command that the Lord gave to His disciples. Where, by God's grace, I have been obedient to His commandments I have put a little check in my Bible and written the word, Hallelujah! Where I have been disobedient, I have confessed my sin, and by His enabling grace have once again committed myself to obey Him and so prove I really do love Him."

Dear reader, once you really 'walk with the Lord in the light of His Word,' you too, will join the hymn-writer in testifying that there is no other way but to 'trust and *obey*!'

The Response of Faith

The Bible is God's faith builder! And as we are built up in faith—which is dependence on, and obedience to, the Lord Jesus Christ—we will affirm 'I can't' but 'He can'!

So in your time together with the Lord, it is good to ask: Is there in this verse—

A promise to claim?
A warning to heed?

The Bible is full of promises. When we meditate upon God's Word, it is necessary to claim the promises of God. At the same time, however, we must also observe His somber warnings. To heed the promises of God, while ignoring the warnings of God is not to 'live by faith'; instead, it is to 'die by make-believe'!

As you read the Bible day by day, notice each promise of God and then claim each one as your very own. Whenever you appropriate God's promises, the enabling sufficiency of the Lord Jesus Christ will be all the power you need to turn every new step of obedience into the reality of your own personal experience.

His promises are given to you to become 'living' truth in your walk with God. As you lay hold of these promises, your faith will continually be strengthened, for we are told: *So then faith comes by hearing, and hearing by the Word of God (Romans 10:17).*

Have you ever wondered what is the opposite of faith? The answer is not so simple as it may seem. To say that unbelief is the opposite of faith really avoids the full implications of this question. Imagine, if you will, three life-giving 'cousins'. The first is faith, the second is dependence, the third is humility. Now, think of three deadly 'cousins'. The first is unbelief, the second is independence and the third is pride.

A man of faith is a man who depends upon the Lord Jesus Christ to do what he could never do for himself. When reading the Bible, the man of real faith will notice, and then personally appropriate, the unbreakable promises of God.

The Lord Jesus said to His disciples: *for without Me you can do nothing (John 15:5)*. Yes, before a person can trust the Lord to do anything of spiritual value through His enabling, he must be convinced that in his own strength he can do nothing that will count for eternity. This kind of dependent faith is only born in a humble heart. Such a person will then be able to say with the apostle Paul *"I can do all things through Christ who strengtheneth me" (Philippians 4:13)*.

A man of unbelief, on the other hand, is a man who considers himself to be so independent that he does not really need the help of God. Sad to say, there are millions today who will not depend upon the Lord Jesus Christ for their salvation. Equally sad is the fact that many Christians do not depend upon the indwelling Christ to enable them to live the Christian life. Any form of human independence is born in a proud, unyielding heart.

So we can say that the opposite of faith is pride, whereas the opposite of unbelief is humility. In spite of popular thinking, self-confidence and self-sufficiency always inoculate the heart against a good dose of faith.

Every worldly influence that is designed to inflate the ego will at the same time deflate one's confident trust in the supernatural power of the risen Christ.

God's limitless resources are behind every promise that He has ever made, and He has not left us to our own devices or cleverness to journey through life.

G. K. Chesterton (1874-1936) astutely put his finger on the paradox of self-sufficient pride. He wrote:

> What we suffer today is modesty in the wrong place. Modesty has settled upon the organ of conviction, where it was never meant to be. A man was meant to be doubtful about himself, but undoubting about the truth; this has been exactly reversed.

Any Christian who remains dependent upon the human counsel of other people, or places confidence in himself rather than in the Lord, will never enter into the fullness of God's blessing. Just as water always runs to the lowest level, so, too, the Holy Spirit, whom Jesus described as *living water,* will not flow to the person whose *soul . . . is lifted up . . . he is a proud man' (Habukkuk 2:4-5 KJ).*

However, the Holy Spirit will overflow in abundance from the heart of any believer who humbly recognizes his need of Christ's enabling power.

> *On the last day, that great day of the feast, Jesus stood and cried out, saying, "If anyone thirsts, let*

him come to Me and drink. He who believes in Me,
as the Scripture has said, out of his heart will flow
*rivers of **living water**" (John 7:37-38).*

Each day you can fall at the feet of Jesus and drink of that living water. As you do, your life will no longer be explained by your talents or training; instead, your life will be characterized by the abundant outflow of God's Holy Spirit from your innermost being.

Remember that in the Person of the Holy Spirit our risen Lord has condescended to clothe Himself with the physical form of every born-again child of God. In fact, today the believer is the strategic beachhead of the Lord Jesus into a godless world. Through each available Christian the Holy Spirit continues to extend His own saving work to the lives of other people.

For you are the temple of the living God. As God has
said: "I will dwell in them, and walk among them I
will be their God, and they shall be my people"
(2 Corinthians 6:16).

Yes, we are God's temples through whom He desires to demonstrate His own holiness and glory!

Recognizing this astonishing fact, Paul continues with the somber exhortation: ***Therefore, having these promises**, beloved, let us cleanse ourselves from all filthiness* *of the flesh and spirit, perfecting holiness in the fear of God (2 Corinthians 7:1).*

Reality in Worship

A tuning fork is the universal tool of a piano tuner. With the fixed pitch of the tuning fork an out-of-tune piano can be restored to perfect harmony.

Likewise, the Bible is God's tool to attune the saddest strain of the human heart to the music and harmony of heaven. And as the Word of God brings fresh insights into the glory, the holiness and the love of God, you will constantly be renewed in your worship and praise by: *Speaking unto yourselves in psalms and spiritual songs, singing and making melody in your hearts to the Lord (Ephesians 5:19 KJ).*

Bearing this in mind, in your time together with the Lord, it is good to ask: Is there in this verse—

A fresh thought about God the Father?
A fresh thought about God the Son?
A fresh thought about God the Holy Spirit?

It is encouraging to observe that today there seems to be a new desire among God's people to truly worship the Lord. The Lord Jesus Christ encouraged such worship when He said: *God is Spirit, and those who worship Him* **must worship in spirit and truth** *(John 4:24).* In other words, true worship must be under the anointing of the Holy Spirit and according to the truth of the Word of God. Only this kind of worship will bring joy to our Father's heart.

When the Holy Spirit draws attention to the wonders of God's Person—His love, His power, His holiness, His glory, His grace, His goodness and any other facet of His beauty—our hearts will be drawn out in a new song of worship and praise to the Lord. A kneeling posture can certainly assist us to cultivate the right attitude of mind when we come to God in prayer. But you may discover with me that there are those very special private moments in your life when kneeling does not seem to be low enough for you to express your love and submission to Him.

It is interesting to note that when John came into the presence of the glorified Christ on the Isle of Patmos, he testified that he did not just kneel but that *when I saw Him, I fell at His feet as dead (Revelation 1:17).*

However, it is important to understand that whenever something is precious to the believer, there is often a dangerous counterfeit close at hand! The Lord Jesus Christ not only gave instruction for true worship, but He also gave a somber warning concerning an activity which, although some would call it worship, is actually a counterfeit of the real thing. At the time He encouraged the Samaritan woman to worship in *'spirit and in truth,'* the Lord Jesus pointedly observed: *You worship what you **do not know** (John 4:22).*

Worship is more than emotion; it must have as its focus the Person of the Lord Jesus Christ. If the purpose of worship is to turn people on rather than to turn them around, then false worship has replaced genuine worship. Surely, the Lord requires more than spiritual excitement if we are to be filled with praise to our God.

True worship is the mind and heart humbly focusing upon the Sovereign, Living Lord Jesus Christ as He is revealed in the Word of God. Whenever this happens, there will be an inner falling down before Him in both surrender and praise.

Alerted to the Adversary

Yes, God is blessing your *Together Time*. Your conscience is now clean. Acknowledging what Jesus has done for you at the Cross, you have renounced your 'right' to yourself, to your reputation, to your ambitions and to your possessions. You are now engaged in a new dimension of worship and praise to the Lord. Are you therefore at the pinnacle of God's purposes of blessing for your *Together Time*? Well, not quite!

There is an enemy out there who is very angry. Yes, the devil is angry because God has provided a way through which He can justly forgive your sin, but the devil is consigned to the Lake of Fire without any possibility of reprieve. Therefore, on your way to heaven, he will do everything he can to dog your footsteps, deflect your devotion to the Lord and destroy your testimony.

> For this reason, in your time together with the Lord, it is good to ask: Is there in this verse—
>
> A fresh insight into the person of Satan?
> A fresh insight into his cruel goals?
> A fresh insight into his subtle devices?

Once I was told about a little boy who returned home from Sunday School. That night his mother noticed him kneeling by his bedside. "What are you doing?" she asked. "I'm making Satan tremble," was the quick reply. "We sang a new hymn at Sunday School today—'Satan trembles when he sees the least of saints upon their knees,' so I got on my knees to make Satan tremble!"

Unfortunately, it takes more to make Satan tremble than just the act of kneeling! Satan only trembles when, in the Name of Jesus, he is denied a lodging place in your life and when in that same all-powerful Name of Jesus you are used by the Holy Spirit to snatch precious lives from the devil's deadly clutches.

Many Christians feel that if they leave Satan alone he will leave them alone. But they are sadly deluded. For instance, when you come to God in prayer, do you sometimes find yourself reflecting with sorrow upon a past defeat even though it has been confessed and forgiven? Satan will always seek to accuse you of sin that you have sincerely dealt with at the Cross.

When Satan reminds you of your past, remind Satan of his future. Although God has chosen not to remember the sins that He has forgiven, Satan wants to get you to refocus on each and every one, so that you will begin to question the reality of God's loving forgiveness.

Indecision, fear, confusion and despair are the classic symptoms of Satan's efforts to intervene in your walk with God.

Yes, Satan will do anything to rob you of your joy and peace. But, as you read the Bible, God will always enable you to discern where Satan has gained a lodging place in your life. Then with the weapons that the Lord has provided, you must close every door to the devil's impudent intrusion!

In human warfare, there are both defensive and aggressive strategies. No battle was ever won by defensive maneuvers alone. Likewise, in spiritual warfare both defensive and aggressive strategies are essential. Both require the artillery of the Word of God. One of the many encouraging aspects of developing a fruitful *Together Time* is that, when you confront Satan either directly or indirectly, you will be able to quote the very Scriptures you have been reading and so be enabled to pray biblically.

It is wonderful to know that when you pray according to God's Word, you pray according to

God's will! And it is God's will for you to know victory over Satan and his attempts to derail your spiritual life.

Defensive Spiritual Warfare: Do you recall when the Lord Jesus was tempted by Satan? I like to think Jesus had just been having His *Together Time* reading in the book of Deuteronomy. Certainly the Scriptures He quoted in His defense against the devil are found in that book. Three times our Lord quoted the written Word of God: *It is written . . . It is written . . . It is written . . . (Matthew 4: 4,7,10).* It is this temptation of the Lord Jesus that enables us to understand the meaning of the psalmist when he wrote *"Thou hast magnified thy word above all thy name" (Psalm 138:2).* Yes, the mighty artillery of the Word of God sent Satan fleeing from Jesus!

Likewise, if you are to overcome the devil, you, too, must learn how to wield the Bible as your weapon of defensive warfare. When Satan plants his foul suggestions in your mind, your recourse should always be the Word of God. A consistent *Together Time* will ensure that God's Word lives in your heart for such an hour.

The following poem, "The Devil's Tactics," by an unknown author is rooted in this truth as it is recorded in Ephesians, chapter 6.

The Devil's Tactics

I had a battle fierce today
within my place of prayer.
I went to meet, and talk with God,
but I found Satan there.
He whispered, 'You can't really pray;
you lost out long ago.
You might say words while on your knees,
but you can't pray, you know.'

So then I pulled my helmet down,
way down upon my ears;
And found it helped to still his voice,
and helped allay my fears.
I checked my other armour too;
my feet in peace were shod.
My loins with truth were girt about,
my sword; the Word of God.
My righteous breastplate still was on,
my heart's love to protect.
My shield of Faith was all intact;
his fiery darts bounced back.
I called on God in Jesus' name;
and pled the precious Blood,
as Satan sneaked away in shame,
I met and talked with God!

Aggressive Spiritual Warfare: Complete victories, however, require more than mere defensive strategy!

There is a hurting world out there. It is the home of billions of precious people for whom Christ died. Everywhere, men and women are hurting, and many are blinded and bound by Satan. I think Satan knows that his time is short, and for this reason he is making his last dastardly bid to secure a godless eternity for dying people.

Though we read how God has prepared a 'lake of fire' for Satan and his demonic hosts, we must remember that God did not prepare that 'lake of fire' for mankind. No, indeed! It was for all these lost people that Christ died. However, in Satan's anger and hatred of all that is holy and good, he wants to take with him as many souls as possible to join him in his eternal suffering. In this warfare for lost souls, Christ continues *to seek and to save (Luke 19:10)* through Christians who have made themselves available to Him.

Have you ever wondered why otherwise intelligent people can not understand the simple gospel message? In the Bible we are told who it is that confuses their thinking, and why it is so difficult for some unbelievers to become believers:

> *But if our gospel be hidden it is hidden to them that are lost, in whom the god of this age* [Satan] *hath blinded the minds of them who believe not, lest the light of the glorious gospel of Christ, who is the image of God, should shine unto them (2 Corinthians 4:3-4 KJ).*

Who stops the light of God's love and truth from penetrating the mind of an unbeliever? The devil! Do you take this into consideration when you pray for the salvation of men and women? As we pray, we must liberate the minds of unconverted people from the delusion of Satan by calling on the all-powerful Name of Jesus. It is that wonderful, powerful and victorious Name about which Charles Wesley wrote:

> Jesus! the name high over all,
>   In hell, or earth or sky;
> Angels and men before it fall,
>   And demons fear and fly.

Yes! Victory over Satan and over all of his demonic hosts was eternally secured at the Cross of Calvary: *For this purpose the Son of God was manifested, that He might destroy the works of the devil (1 John 3:8).* Hallelujah! We do **not** fight a battle that has been lost. Certainly not! We press home the victory that was irrevocably secured on our behalf two thousand years ago.

In a game of chess it is possible for you to make a decisive, irrevocable move of victory against your opponent. From that point his defeat is assured. But if your opponent is stubborn, even though there is no way he could ever reverse his defeat, he could still delay the moment when he will be vanquished.

So it is with Satan; though there is no way he can possibly ever win his battle, he tries to delay God's pre-determined time of his ultimate banishment as long as possible. Thank God that in the remaining brief period of time before Satan will be bound in chains, he is not only a **defeated foe** but he is also a **discovered foe**. The Bible tells us that: *We are not ignorant of his devices (2 Corinthians 2:11)*. To know the strategy of the enemy is to gain the advantage in battle!

The Apostle John recorded the victory of saints who overcame the devil, and the means whereby the Lord's victory became theirs: *they overcame him* [the Devil] *by the blood of the Lamb, and by the word of their testimony; and they loved not their lives unto the death (Revelation 12:11 KJ)*. We do not love our lives to the death, because already *our old man was crucified with Him (Romans 6:6)*.

Yes, it is the cleansing of the Blood, the confession of our lips and our co-crucifixion with Christ that spell our title deed to victory in Jesus over the powers of hell. Hallelujah!

Rejoice with me; the Lord Jesus has made every provision for us to become mature, 'over-coming' Christians. But at the same time we must beware that if we have no desire to stretch beyond the kindergarten class in the things of God, the Lord will never force spiritual maturity upon us. Our spiritual capacity for Him is determined in the context of time while we are here on earth, and, according to how much we mature in the Lord, that capacity will be enjoyed forever in unclouded and intimate fellowship with Him when we arrive in Heaven.

Spiritual Check-up

1. What do I think about as I go to sleep?
2. When I read the Bible am I expecting to hear from God?
3. When I read the Bible am I willing to act upon what God says?
4. Is my life still explained in terms of 'me' or is it explained in terms of Christ who lives in me *(Galatians 2:20)*?
5. Am I an independent person? If so, am I willing to renounce my pride and exercise total dependence upon God?
6. Do I realize that adoration of my God is the highest activity in which I can engage?
7. Has Satan found a lodging place in my life?
8. Do I need personally to appropriate the victory of Christ over Satan?

*My faith has found a resting
place, Not in device nor creed:
I trust the Ever living One,
His wounds for me shall plead.*

*My heart is leaning on the Word,
The written Word of God,
Salvation by my Savior's name,
Salvation through His blood.*

*I need no other argument,
I need no other plea,
It is enough that Jesus died,
And that he died for me.*

Lidie H. Edmunds

CHAPTER 5

The Faith Factor

Picture in your mind a man confronted with the task of crossing a turbulent river to reach his friend on the other side. He has no boat; just a kite, and several pieces of string, each one a little stronger than the previous one until the final piece is as strong as a rope. Using the thinnest string, the man flies his kite and maneuvers it so that it will land in the hands of his friend on the other side of the river. To the original kite string, he now attaches the next stronger piece, and then an even stronger piece until the rope itself has been stretched across the impassable river. After the rope has been tied to a tree on both sides, the man is then able to safely cross the river to reach his friend.

As a born-again child of God, you have already placed your faith in the death of the Lord Jesus Christ as God's loving substitute for your sins. But as you begin to read the Bible, your faith may be just as weak as that first piece of string—but even that was enough to maintain contact with the kite as it crossed the river! However, since *faith comes by hearing, and hearing by the word of God (Romans 10:17),* you will discover that as you continue to read God's Word and lay hold of His precious promises, your faith will grow stronger. God purposes that each of His children be strong in faith, which presupposes a close, 'together' relationship between the child of God and his Heavenly Father.

In the Bible, Jude records just how necessary it is to build upon that initial foundation of saving faith: *But you, beloved, building yourselves up **on** your most holy faith . . . (Jude 20).*

The Amplified Bible transliterates the idea this way:

*But you, beloved, build yourselves up [founded] on your most holy faith [make progress, rise like an edifice higher and higher] **praying in the Holy Spirit; guard and keep yourselves in the love of God; expect and patiently wait for the mercy of our Lord Jesus Christ** (the Messiah)—[which will bring you] unto life eternal . . . And on some **have mercy** who waver and doubt. [Strive to] **save others**, snatching [them] out of [the] fire; on others take pity [but] with fear, loathing even the garment spotted by the flesh and polluted by their sensuality (Jude 20-23 AMP).*

These verses stress that on the sure foundation of saving faith we are to build ourselves up spiritually (*i.e.*, to mature and reinforce our faith) **by developing**

a life of prayer; love; living hope; active compassion and earnest soul-winning.

Even as your salvation was received as a free gift through faith, so too, when by faith you appropriate the all-sufficient life of the risen Lord, you will be controlled by the indwelling Christ. Yes, *the just shall live by faith (Romans 1:17; Galatians 3:11; Hebrews 10:38).* Whether in Heaven or while you are still on earth, you must live by faith—live by trusting God and His promises, and by being available for Him to do His work through you. Even when you get to Heaven, your faith will be the avenue whereby you will gladly and gratefully rejoice in God's eternal purposes of love, which will go far beyond anything your redeemed mind will ever be able to comprehend.

While you are still on earth, genuine faith must be constantly dependent on the Lord Jesus Christ to do **in you**, and **through you**, what you could never otherwise accomplish. As God's children, it is imperative for each one of us to grow in faith; we must learn to increasingly depend upon the Giver of Life and the Designer of our daily walk.

Too often, however, we resort to our human reasoning, which would endeavor to substitute any number of things for genuine faith. Our human independence will try to replace faith with enthusiastic, even sacrificial service for the Lord. Yet, true living faith is not necessarily evidenced by the Christian's loyalty to a program, by his commitment to a preacher, or even by his dedication to acquiring comprehensive knowledge of the contents of the

Bible. Though such commitments can sometimes reflect genuine faith, they can also be used, intentionally or unintentionally, as a deadly, self-driven substitute for dynamic and personal faith.

True faith is directly related to our expectant dependence upon the risen Lord Jesus Christ. Unfortunately, many Christians think they can succeed in life by using their talents, or by employing their manipulative personalities, or even by depending on the resources in their bank account; but the Bible clearly tells us that as born-again believers, in order to succeed, our lives must be controlled by the Holy Spirit. If we do not exercise dependent faith in God, the Scriptures declare that all of our work that we so foolishly substitute for His enabling power will eventually be lost. Our effectiveness as Christians will not be determined by how **enthusiastic** we are in what we do ourselves, but whether or not true faith has been the motivating source of all our activities.

Anything in your life apart from God's love that gives you a sense of security or significance—be it your money, or your education, or your friends, or your power, or your job, or even your physical appearance—is an indication that you are not living by faith. Your only true security and significance in life must be found in your God and your Redeemer. If you do not so live by faith during your earthly pilgrimage, you will have been deprived of the continual joy of God's presence in your life and of His ministry of love through you. For *whatever is not from faith is sin (Romans 14:23).*

Truly, G. Keith expressed his understanding of the importance of feeding on God's Word to stimulate faith when he wrote:

> How firm a foundation,
>   Ye saints of the Lord,
> Is laid for your faith
>   In His excellent Word.

Without the Voice of God realized in our hearts and lives, there can be no foundation for spiritual growth, and there can be no mortar for this foundation unless we follow the divine plan for spending time alone with the Savior, together with Him in intimate communion and fellowship.

Faith is the dynamic that generates living fellowship with God.

A number of years ago I remember speaking on the theme of revival to some one hundred pastors in the United Kingdom. God had been working among us with great power and heart-searching. Leading into a time of public prayer, one pastor rose to his feet, and with heart-stirred brokenness and watery eyes prayed something like this: "O God, I confess that so often when I have previously led in prayer before these brethren, I have been more conscious of them and of sound theology than of Your Holy Presence . . ."

Our hearts are so deceptive that even when we pray, it is possible that we are hiding behind our own words rather than sincerely attempting to expose our true hearts needs before our Father in Heaven. To recite a prayer, or to 'say our prayers,' does not necessarily mean that we truly pray. And only when our hearts are openly attuned to Him in the transparency of His eternal light and holiness does our Lord receive divine pleasure from our time of fellowship.

It is an awesome thought to think that a needy sinner could bring any sense of satisfaction to a Holy God. But the Bible tells us that God created mankind for that very purpose: to bring glory to Himself. Whether we like it or not, each one of us exists for the glory of a Holy God!

That you may have a walk worthy of the Lord, **fully pleasing** *Him (Colossians 1:10)* was the earnest desire of the apostle Paul for the Church at Colossae. Bishop Handley Moule translated the phrase fully pleasing as being *"unto every anticipation of His will."* That is probably what we mean when we say 'please yourself'. By this expression we convey our desire for the preference of the will of another before our own will.

To try to please ourselves rather than to seek to please our God will mean that we are destined to stub our toes on every rock, knock our head against every wall and trip over every obstacle along the pathway of life. But what joy there is in the heart of every believer, and in the heart of God Himself, when the child of God communes with his Creator in the transparent light of His glory and love!

The Bible helpfully reveals that there is a definite connection between 'faith' and 'pleasing God'. The negative grammatical structure in which the following verse is written makes the connection between faith and pleasing God even more emphatic: *But without faith it is impossible to please Him . . .* This verse then shifts into a positive statement which surely brings great encouragement to every genuine believer. It tells us that 'fellowship' with God results in 'rewards' from God: *. . . for he who **comes to God** must believe that He is, and that He is a **rewarder** of those who diligently seek Him (Hebrews 11:6).*

The spiritual rewards that God graciously bestows upon the person who lives in intimate fellowship with his Savior and Lord are utterly inexpressible; they can only be understood when personally experienced. And the key to living fellowship with God, which will bring Him pleasure and His children great joy, is **faith**.

Yes, *faith* is the vehicle through which the Holy Spirit relays the victory of the risen Lord to the child of God.

As we have noted, it is quite possible, sad to say, for us to be exposed to the promises of God, either through listening to a preacher or by reading God's Word, and still find it is of no spiritual profit: *but the Word . . . did not profit them, not being mixed with faith (Hebrews 4:2).*

Only as the Word of God is stirred down from the head to the heart with the mixing spoon of faith, will the reading of God's Word become profitable. It is at that point that the Holy Spirit applies the enabling grace of the Lord Jesus Christ to our lives, so that we are able to grasp each opportunity to serve the Lord, and so that we will prove **His** enabling power to face every problem of life.

One thing is certain, however; every true believer will experience days of severe trial and temptation. Satan himself will constantly use 'the world' with its enticing overtures to deflect us from a life of day-by-day fellowship with our Lord. Nothing is more heinous to Satan than the child of God who is in vital communion with his Redeemer and Lord. Therefore, it is not surprising that the Evil One will go to any length to estrange born-again Christians from their Creator in order to keep them from experiencing faith-building *Together Times*.

To the spiritually-naive person, the material world appears to be the only reality of life. But just the opposite is true; in fact, it is the spiritual world that embraces ultimate reality. *For all that is in the world, the lust of the flesh, and the lust of the eyes, and the pride of life, is not of the Father, but is of the world (1 John 2:16 KJ)*. Because people are so easily deceived, the devil has little difficulty employing his dastardly devices to seduce the Christian.

The Bible tells us that we are tempted through the lust of the flesh (pleasure without responsibility); the lust of the eyes (possessions without responsibility); and the pride of life (power without responsibility). Satan knows all the tricks of interfering with what God has planned for us; he will do anything to keep us from being together with our Lord. The Wicked One knows that when we are in such intimate contact with our God we will grow spiritually and thereby bring our Heavenly Father increased pleasure.

The Lust of the Flesh: It is through today's blatantly immoral world, which is so obviously saturated with sexual pollution, that Satan incites the lustful appetite of the flesh. Our enemy finds ready access to the lives of people who are absorbed with the sensual, the physical and the material. However, those who have been deceived by Satan's evil suggestions all too soon find that the bubble of sin's pleasure has burst leaving nothing but a sense of emptiness and shame!

The Lust of the Eyes: If we are attracted by the slick world of commercialism and if we envy what other people possess, Satan is able to make his cruel advances. The Great Deceiver whispers, "If only you had a new watch, an acre of land, or a bigger home, you would be happy." But because: . . . *man shall not live by bread alone, but by every word that proceeds from the mouth of God (Matthew 4:4),* we soon discover, after having indulged ourselves in our latest whims, that our new acquisitions bring us no lasting satisfaction.

The Pride of Life: The door for Satan's destructive maneuvers is also opened wide by our arrogance, egotism and false sense of self-sufficiency. God hates pride in any form!

After all, having confidence in our own ability to control our destiny is the opposite of faith—for **faith** is confidence in the Lord Jesus. And as we have already noted God has said that the only answer to the pride of life is to: *humble yourselves in the sight of the Lord (James 4:10).* Humbly acknowledging your dependence upon Almighty God is the one way you can close the door to Satan when he subtly suggests that you are self-sufficient. And your dependence— which is faith—will give you victory for: ***this is the victory that has overcome the world even our faith*** *(1 John 5:4 KJ).*

But, before you can **fully** enter into the victory of overcoming-faith (when Satan approaches you through all that is in the world), it is also important for you to learn a lesson that the Lord Jesus taught His disciples. He warned them of yet another great hindrance to genuine faith. ***How can you believe,*** Jesus asked, *who receive honor from one another, and do not seek the honor that comes from the only God (John 5:44)?* In these words the Lord Jesus solemnly pointed out to His disciples that faith will never co-exist with a subtle desire to receive the praise and adulation of other people. And it is approbation lust that is a big problem to many Christian people. However, the approval of a Christ-rejecting society is no mark of genuine Christian discipleship.

When you enjoy your daily *Together Time*, your faith will grow. Then later when you face the testings and opportunities of life, you will know how to exercise that vibrant and overcoming-faith.

Spiritual Check-up

1. In my daily activities, do I enjoy a faith that functions?
2. Do I see a problem in every opportunity or an opportunity, to prove the sufficiency of Christ, in every problem?
3. Do I want God's cause to advance or is it my desire to advance His cause myself?
4. Is my life panic-proof because I reflect a day-by-day dependence upon the Lord?

Lord, speak to me, that I may speak
In living echoes of Thy tone;
As Thou hast sought, so let me seek
Thy erring children, lost and lone.

O teach me, Lord, that I may teach
The precious things Thou dost impart;
And wing my words, that they may reach
The hidden depths of many a heart.

O fill me with Thy fullness, Lord,
Until my very heart o'erflow
In kindling thought and glowing word,
Thy love to tell, Thy praise to show.

Frances Ridley Havergal

CHAPTER 6

Time to Tell

One night after I had been speaking at a service, a father came to me and asked if I would pray for him. God had been with us in unusual power. The father told me that he had a problem witnessing to colleagues and friends. As I often do when seeking to help somebody, I silently asked the Lord for discernment as to what was the real need in this man's life. I found myself replying, "I don't think that's the real problem. Would you kneel with me now and ask God to show you why you have a problem with witnessing?" Without hesitation, the father knelt and prayed.

As he did so, it seemed to me that the Lord Himself was exposing a deeper problem than that of silent lips. With great brokenness, my friend was telling the Lord what a tyrant he had been in his home and particularly how dictatorial he had been in regard to his children. With heartfelt repentance, he asked the Lord for forgiveness.

That night we never did discuss his problem in witnessing, for Jesus had revealed Himself to this father in a new and living way. The following night, he came to the meeting with a radiant face, and joyfully told me, "I haven't been able to keep quiet all day telling others about Jesus!"

Nowhere in the Bible are we told to present a contrived 'plan of salvation' to unconverted people! However, we are exhorted to walk in constant fellowship with the Lord Jesus Christ so that, when we do share the gospel message with them, the overflow of His love through us will incline their hearts to hear the truth of the Word of God.

However, on those days when our hearts are **not** attuned to Him in living fellowship, we will discover our witness is **not** significantly effective and fruitful. In fact, on such days our lips will be sealed from sharing the Word of God with other people, and we will be unable to spontaneously reveal the Lord to the Christ-rejecting world around us.

Beginning each day with God in a vital *Together Time* is the first step in helping you to rid yourself of those inhibitions which so easily intrude when you have the opportunity to **tell** unconverted people about the Lord Jesus Christ. There is a vast difference between genuinely experiencing a spiritually fruitful life in a godless world, and that of being a 'gospel salesman'! No, the believer is not commissioned to stand up in the world to say certain words that **seem** to bear witness to Christ. Instead, the born-again Christian can be assured that he is already **in** Christ, and from that position he will gladly talk of Jesus.

As the Lord said to His disciples: *He that abideth* ***in me,*** *and I* ***in him,*** *the same bringeth forth much fruit: for without Me ye can do nothing (John 15:5).* Abiding in Him and telling others of Him are your responsibilities; the fruit is His responsibility!

After the day of Pentecost, the disciples could not contain their enthusiasm and joy, having already personally walked and talked with their risen Lord. Everywhere they went they told people—even those who were hostile to the person of Christ—about the *wonderful works of God (Acts 2:11).* Their hearers' curiosity was aroused, and as a result thousands of people gathered to hear Peter publicly preach on the theme of the Lordship of Christ. And as He preached, a deep conviction of personal sin fell upon the congregation. The very people who had recently been responsible for crucifying Christ bewailed: *Men and brethren, what shall we do? (Acts 2:37).* On that day the personal testimony of the disciples and the public preaching of Peter combined to reap a great harvest of souls!

Later, while living in an adversarial environment, the disciples again met with God in a vital prayer meeting. 'Religious' men who hated both the disciples and their message had told them to stop talking about Jesus. Earlier on, in the Upper Room, the Lord Jesus had not taught a course on personal evangelism to instruct the disciples how to witness; however, because they were now filled with the Holy

Spirit, these enthusiastic Christians spontaneously responded: *We cannot but speak the things which we have seen and heard (Acts 4:20).* They had again been in the presence of God! Their hearts were burning with the reality of the risen Christ. They could not keep silent!

In the early sixties, Dorothy and I ministered behind what was then called 'The Iron Curtain'. In answer to an inquiry about the difficulties of pastoring under a totalitarian regime, a faithful pastor replied: "We are fewer in number now, but at least we know who we are. Those of us who remain know the risen Christ and we are invincible." (Such testings are already the experience of some of my readers, but the way things are going, if the Lord Jesus does not quickly return, many of the rest of us will also be called upon to venture all for Christ in ways we never thought possible.)

Dorothy recently recorded in her *Together Time* notebook: "But the cost of His death must be felt with each breath if His Spirit would flow through me." Certainly the early disciples paid a great price for their bold witness. But when they were threatened with imprisonment for talking about Jesus, they met together for prayer. We read: *They were all filled with the Holy Spirit, and they spoke the word of God with boldness (Acts 4:31).*

Effective evangelism results from overflow—the overflow of the Holy Spirit from the life of the

Spirit-filled believer, thus revealing to others, the reality of the indwelling Christ.

As we read the New Testament, we notice that evangelism in the early church was not only the result of a persuasive platform personality. There would have been no crowds to hear Peter preach on the Day of Pentecost if the disciples had not first gone forth to personally proclaim *the wonderful works of God (Acts 2:11)*.

When the purity, the life and the love of the Lord Jesus Christ flow from a believer's heart to a despairing world, people are softened and made ready to hear God's truth. That is why we need to meet the Lord each day in the light of His Word so as to be constantly *filled with the Spirit (Ephesians 5:18)*.

Overflow Evangelism

In the early days of my Christian life, I was part of a fellowship of young people. We certainly possessed more 'enthusiasm' than 'knowledge'! In spite of this (or maybe because of this!) God saw fit to use us among our unconverted friends. Let me relate a few of these experiences in which, as young believers, we became involved.

Vocational life: At the time of my conversion I was working and studying in the Civil Engineer's Office of the Town Council. Working in the Town Hall, I was one day summoned to the plush offices of the

Town Clerk! There I was severely admonished: "I have heard of your 'extra-curricular' activities," said this boss of bosses. He was obviously referring to the evangelistic services that we young people were conducting. Each night, just after the public houses had closed, we held open-air evangelistic services at a popular gathering place in the town. To begin with, the passers-by would not readily stop to listen so we were often glad when somebody began to heckle the speaker. As the antagonist gave him a hard time, other people joined him, while yet others gathered to support 'the poor man on the soap-box.' Before long we would have quite a crowd to preach to, and on some nights one or two people would make a profession of coming to the Savior! The Town Clerk warned me that such 'fanaticism' must not be associated in any way with the professional prestige of the Town Hall! He strongly warned me to cease all such activity. But since the open-air meetings seemed to be bearing fruit, all of us young people felt led to continue!

Later, when attending Bible College, I remember our College President saying in the weekly chapel service: "If you can't hold a crowd in the open-air, don't bore a captive audience in a church!" When I heard this, I was again thankful that we young people had persisted with our open-air evangelism!

Immediately after my conversion, I had testified to all my professional colleagues about my new faith in Christ. But then I remembered one person associated with the office to whom I had not had an opportunity to witness. It was the lady who came each night to scrub the dirty floors. One night after my colleagues had left, I located the scrub brushes and buckets. Soon, the floors were clean and I waited for the scrublady to arrive. "Your work is done," I joyfully exclaimed. After a stunned silence, she sat with me over a cup of tea. Of course, in our conversation I was able to tell her about Jesus. I will always remember the tears that flowed from her eyes as we talked and prayed together.

Social life: I also recall my twenty-first birthday, which in those days was always a very special occasion in England. Such an event was often celebrated with a big dinner followed by a dance. But by the time I was twenty-one, God had already taken the dance out of my feet and put it into my heart. So I saw my twenty-first birthday party, which my parents so lovingly provided, as yet another opportunity to win my friends to Christ. Accordingly, I invited an evangelist for the occasion! The invitation cards to my unconverted business associates and friends explained that a friend of mine would be giving a speech after the meal! "Your **presence** and not your **presents** is requested" was the indelicate invitation on that card. And on that night, one of my friends was wonderfully converted!

Later, when I became Assistant Pastor at a Baptist Church in London, the young people never organized a trip down the river, a ramble through the country, or a sports evening without making the occasion attractive enough to invite unconverted friends. Without exception, they ended every such activity with a solid gospel presentation. Why not? The young people recognized that the purpose for the existence of their Young People's Fellowship was firstly to build themselves up in the Lord and secondly to see their friends converted to Christ. It is little wonder, then, that the Young People's Fellowship flourished under the blessing of God.

Spiritual life: I had never been interested in seriously studying the Bible before I was converted at the age of nineteen. Consequently, at that age I knew very little about God's Word. But after I had accepted Christ as my Lord and Savior, every Monday night a few of us new converts would gather in a home to study the Bible together. Our enthusiastic motivation was to get God's Word through our heads and into our hearts as quickly as possible! Even in those early days we conducted our Bible studies in the basic way that I have already suggested in this book. No, we did not look upon God's Word as a religious textbook, but rather regarded it as a compass to guide us through life.

As the direct result of those simple Bible studies, a few other young people were converted and together we conceived ways to carry the gospel message further afield. Because none of us owned a car, we hit on the idea of making a bicycle trailer. One or two of the fellows who were mechanically-minded also engineered an amplifying system, complete with a wind-up 'gramophone'. On some of our weekends, we would cycle out to the surrounding villages, towing our trailer and amplifier behind us.

I well remember the particular village where the Methodist Church had been closed and its doors securely locked. In our enthusiasm for spreading the gospel, we located the keys, obtained permission to use the building, polished the dust off the pews, and then proceeded to the Village Green with our amplifying system. Outside the 'village pub' we established our pulpit and began an open-air meeting by playing a brand new record of an American soloist Bev Shea. He had just visited England with a young man by the name of Billy Graham, who had recently made his first appearance in the country. In between the gospel songs, we took turns standing on the soap-box and giving personal testimonies of our faith in Christ as Savior and Lord. After a short while, some of us tried to preach to the curious people who came out of the pub to listen to us on the green. To the amazement of the villagers, the Lord saw fit to nicely fill the church by the end of the weekend. A future Sunday School teacher found Christ, and later her sister also came to the Savior. Soon, the doors were no longer locked and a little Sunday School and weekly church services recommenced.

Paul charged Timothy: *Preach the word; be diligent in season, out of season . . . (2 Timothy 4:2 KJ)*. If Paul were ministering today, he would probably have spoken to Timothy in words something like these: "If there is an opportunity to share God's Word, take it; if there isn't an opportunity, make it! There never is a season when it is inopportune to preach the Word!" I am sure Paul would look unfavorably on any kind of formal Bible study in which the acquired knowledge of the student did not later extend, in loving and courageous ways, to people who would never darken the door of a church.

When you have learned the secret of getting the Word of God from your head to your heart, you will discover that it will not take long for God's Word to become, in the words of Jeremiah, *fire in your bones*.

Sadly, if the Bible only remains in your head, it is tragically possible for you to be a man of the Word yet not a man of the Spirit. There will be no fire in your bones! But as you meet God regularly in your *Together Time*, you will realize more and more that it is impossible for you to be a man of the Spirit without at the same time being a man of the Word!

Yes, God does speak to us when we read His Word, and what He says He expects us to share with others. God said to Ezekiel: *Therefore you shall hear a word from My mouth and warn them for Me (Ezekiel 33:7)*. But there is no use speaking to others unless we have first heard, and then personally responded to, the words from His mouth.

There are many 'advocates' of Christianity, but, unfortunately, there are too few who are able to bear genuine witness of their personal relationship with the Living God.

Later, from his own experience, the Apostle John was able to joyfully testify of the reality of his living fellowship with Christ. Therefore, as we would expect, he then invited others to join him in this intimate fellowship: *. . . that you also may have fellowship with us; and truly our fellowship is with the Father and with His Son Jesus Christ (1 John 1:3).*

Spiritual Check-up

1. Do I recognize both the place where I work and the place where I live as my personal mission field?
2. Do I see people merely as candidates for conversion, or do I prayerfully seek to love them to new-life in Christ?
3. When did I last earn the right to witness for Christ by helping somebody in a practical way?
4. Are my lips sealed from talking boldly of Jesus because:
   My life is compromised?
   My career might be in jeopardy?
   My pride is unwilling to line up with the despised and rejected Jesus of Nazareth?

Eternal Light

Eternal Light! Eternal Light!
How pure the soul must be,
When, placed within Thy searching sight,
It shrinks not, but, with calm delight,
Can live, and look on Thee!

The spirits that surround Thy throne
May bear the burning bliss;
But that is surely theirs alone,
Since they have never, never known
A fallen world like this.

O how shall I, whose native sphere
Is dark, whose mind is dim,
Before the Ineffable appear,
And on my naked spirit bear
The uncreated beam?

There is a way for man to rise
To that sublime abode:
An offering and a sacrifice,
A Holy Spirit's energies,
An Advocate with God.

These, these prepare us for the sight
Of holiness above:
The sons of ignorance and night
May dwell in the eternal Light,
Through the eternal Love!

Thomas Binney (1798–1874)

CHAPTER 7

Fruit or Fire

A friend of mine called Bengt was a Swedish-American who had immigrated to the United States. There he became a successful Christian businessman. Among his several ministries, Bengt delighted in transporting missionary airplanes to their destination on mission fields. One year, he and a friend of his were asked to take a small plane to Alaska for Mission Aviation Fellowship (M.A.F.). Having completed the bulk of their journey, his friend left him at Fairbanks airport, and Bengt prepared to fly solo the final lap of the journey.

Just before leaving, Bengt's friend tossed an emergency pack into the small plane. It consisted of one bar of chocolate and a warm blanket. During this last leg of the flight, a storm unexpectedly sprang up. The treacherous winds in the Alaskan mountain range sucked the tiny aircraft into a down-draft. Flipping upside down, the plane skidded to a halt at the edge of a mountain cliff. For the next three days snow fell, but in the goodness of God the wind blew the snow off the white underbelly of the plane, keeping it from being covered. However, because the white underbelly was surrounded by snow, when the U.S. Coast Guard air search rescue teams flew overhead, Bengt's little plane was not noticed.

After the military called off their air search rescue teams, Bengt's son Bruce, a fine young Christian man, together with a M.A.F. pilot, asked the Lord to guide them to Bengt. Meanwhile on the ground, Bengt had become increasingly weak and had even taken a delayed action photograph of himself, which showed him waving goodbye to his loved ones with a gaunt, yet smiling face. However, God had other plans. As Bruce and his friend flew over the site of the downed plane, the reflection of the sun on the white metal underbelly drew their searching eyes to Bengt's location.

Why do I recount this story? Later Bengt told me that during those ten days he was living at the brink of the Judgment Seat of Christ. When I next saw him, he told me that when he had been alone with God on that snowy mountain cliff, the Holy Spirit had permitted him to review his life on earth as he anticipated his soon home-call into the presence of God. He said it was as if the 'Judgment Seat of Believers' had come to him ahead of time. As his life spread out before him, Bengt reflected upon his years of dedicated Christian service and wondered how much of it would really count for eternity.

With great seriousness, Bengt told me that he came to realize that the church board meetings, the missionary council meetings and his many church activities, though gladly undertaken, he had really done in the energy of his flesh, in the expression of his own talents and abilities, and not as a result of the overflow of the fullness of the Holy Spirit.

Bengt said that in those ten days God had shown him that such 'worthwhile' activities were just 'wood, hay and stubble', (the metaphors used in the Bible to refer to those days and deeds in our lives which will be burned up at the Judgment Seat for Believers and therefore not count for eternity).

That awesome experience for Bengt was really a revival experience in his life. Those of us who loved him and had known him for so long and had so appreciated the zeal with which he had thrown himself into the work of God later came to understand what he had meant, for his remaining few years were explained, not in terms of his own abilities and strength, but in terms of a new surge of the overflow of God's blessing and power through his life wherever he witnessed.

It is a sober thought for Christians to remember that we shall appear at the Judgment Seat prepared for **all believers**. This Judgment Seat must be distinguished from The Great White Throne of Judgment. The Great White Throne is the place where **all unbelievers** will be judged and condemned to a lost eternity, whereas the Judgment Seat of Believers is the place where everything that was not of faith will be burned and everything that was of faith will live forever to the glory of God, because He

Himself has done the work! On that day, many Christians will sadly discover that even their busyness in the church and their popularity in religious circles, which so satisfied them during their lifetime, did not count in the mind of God as genuine spiritual service.

White Pages

I have before me two pieces of clean white paper. Both are blank. No one has either written or drawn on them. If you were to look at them, you would not see anyone's thoughts in print nor any beautiful picture. But at the same time, you would not see somebody's mistakes! Just as there is no beauty, so, too, there are no smudges or blots. **Just white pages; nothing more, nothing less**.

Your life and mine could have many days which are like those white pages. Though once smeared by sin, now, because of the wonderful mercy of God, and through the Atoning Blood of Jesus, every page of life for the believer has been cleansed. Nothing remains but that which is *as white as snow (Isaiah 1:18)*. As I look back upon some of the pages of my life as a Christian, I remember with sadness how, wittingly or unwittingly, through willfulness or through weakness, I have sinned and grieved the Holy Spirit. Except for the Blood of Jesus, those white pages would have been forever blotted with the ugly stains of sin and self-centeredness. What wonderful mercy and grace God has extended to me, so that even those pages which were once so sin-stained are now as white as snow! **White pages; but, praise God, no blots or smudges!**

However, it is a sobering thought for me also to realize that whatever the Holy Spirit has **not** done through me has **not** counted for eternity. In the words of the Apostle Paul, those days of life can be described as having been *saved, yet so as through fire (1 Corinthians 3:15)*. When there has been no overflow of the Holy Spirit from my life, though my sins have been erased by my forgiving Lord, nothing has been accomplished that will count for eternity. **White pages; but, sadly, nothing more!**

Though some of the pages of life will remain forever white, other pages will have recorded on them indelible pictures of exquisite beauty—pages painted by His own nail-pierced hands of love—glorifying Him forever. For every believer, these glorious pages are the record of those days when we have been available vessels through which an eternal God was able to do His eternal work. **Yes, white pages; but, praise God, much more!**

Wasted Years

How tragic it is when those who are daily invited by God to 'come and dine' waste years of their lives that they could instead spend in the joy of ever-deepening fellowship with their Lord and in bringing pleasure to the Savior Himself.

My heart fills with sad joy when I recall an elderly gentleman whose very salvation was sullied by the hurt of lost opportunities and of years wasted on the superficial pleasures of life. Soon after my conversion, together with a few other young people who had also just received Christ, I went to a local hospital to minister. Every other Saturday night, we shared the gospel message and prayed with some of the elderly folk who had no hope of ever leaving their hospital ward. One particular evening, I moved over to the bedside of an elderly man who, as it turned out, would die before our next Saturday night visit.

After having heard our brief Bible message, he was obviously very moved, and, with tears rolling down his face, he falteringly disclosed: "I know I'm saved and going to Heaven." "That's wonderful," I replied. Before I could say anything further, he began sobbing, not with unrestrained joy but with the pain of inner hurt. With a feeble voice, he whispered: "Yes—but not completely—you see I'm seventy-one years old now and seventy years of my life have been wasted!"

As a young convert, what could I reply? I don't remember how I tried to comfort him, but I do remember going home that night, getting on my knees and saying to the Lord something like this: "Lord, even now I am looking into the future on a life that one day I will be looking back on. When it is my time to come to Heaven, I don't want to come with my soul saved but my life wasted. Tonight, I again yield my life to You. I pray You will make it really count for eternity."

In the Old Testament, Habakkuk warned that it is possible to expend a great deal of energy and then later sadly discover that what we have done has amounted to nothing. When he informed the people of his day, *the just shall live by his faith (Habukkuk 2:4),* he also warned them that those who do not apply the faith principle of total dependence on God to activities of life *labor to feed the fire (Habukkuk 2:13).* Because those people established their city completely independent of God, nothing but ashes remained. Similarly, whatever we do that has not been totally dependent upon the Lord Jesus Christ will one day be brought to nothing in the fiery presence of God.

Later in the New Testament, Paul likewise warns:

> *Now if anyone builds on this foundation* [the foundation of the Lord Jesus Christ] *with gold, silver, precious stones, wood, hay, straw, each one's work will become manifest; for the Day will declare it, because it will be revealed by fire; and the fire will test each one's work, of what sort it is. If anyone's work which he has built on it endures, he will receive a reward. If anyone's work is burned, he will suffer loss; but he himself will be saved, yet so as through fire (1 Corinthians 3:12-15).*

The seventy-one year-old gentleman in the nursing home was glad he was saved, but he was also very sad that he was saved—*as through fire*. The fire that would burn the wood, hay and stubble of his life, is the same fire that will purify the gold, silver and precious stones of those through whom the Holy Spirit has been free to build with God's own imperishable building blocks.

Eternal Light

An eternal God will do His eternal work through each Christian who, abiding in Christ, nourishes his faith and applies God's Word to his life. Such believers will be able to face each new day with glad anticipation as they assuredly testify: *Therefore, since we are receiving a kingdom which cannot be shaken, let us have grace, by which we may serve God acceptably with reverence and godly fear (Hebrews 12:28)*. Effective, regular *Together Times* will encourage us to walk in the power of the Holy Spirit, and not in the energy of our flesh.

One day, in the all-searching light of God's Holy Presence, those people who have been available vessels for the work of the Living God will rejoice with exceeding joy. Yes, as we are drawn to His banqueting table day by day, the God of Light and Love invites us to enjoy transparent fellowship with Him. In this way, we will become His channel of light and love to a dark and selfish world.

Spiritual Check-up

1. If I continue to live the way I am living now, will there be any fruit from my life at the Judgment Seat of Christ?
2. When I pray, do I approach God as *Eternal Light* or do I regard Him merely as my personal benefactor in Heaven?
3. Now, do I need to pray the prayer of David: *Revive me according to Thy Word (Psalm 119: 25)?*

Break Thou the bread of life,
dear Lord to me,
As Thou didst break the loaves
beside the sea:
Beyond the sacred page
I seek Thee, Lord;
My spirit pants for Thee,
O living Word.

Thou art the bread of life,
O Lord, to me;
Thy holy Word the truth
that saveth me:
Give me to eat and live
with Thee above;
Teach me to love Thy truth,
for Thou art love.

O send Thy Spirit,
Lord, now unto me,
That He may touch my eyes
and make me see;
Show me the truth concealed
within Thy Word,
And in Thy book revealed
I see the Lord.

Mary Ann Lathbury

CHAPTER 8

Come and Dine

On the sandy shore of the Lake of Galilee stood the risen Son of God, alone and unnoticed. Maybe it was the morning mist that shrouded His majestic presence from the eyes of the weary disciples. Or perhaps, their spiritual eyes had become clouded in the aftermath of Jesus' death upon a cruel cross.

Not far from shore the despairing disciples huddled together in a tiny fishing vessel. They had just spent a frustrating night fishing, during which they had *caught nothing*. As if to add insult to injury, someone asked, *Children, have you any food?* Then, from the lips of that distant person on the shore, there came a clear all-knowing command: *Cast the net on the right side of the boat, and you will find some.*

Awakened from his nightmarish stupor, John responded to the familiar voice and joyfully exclaimed: *It is the Lord!* With renewed hope, the disciples obeyed their Lord's directives, and immediately the net was filled with a great catch of fish! Then, in his enthusiasm, Peter plunged into the waves and eagerly swam to his Master *(John 21:11)*.

On the shore, none other than the risen Lord of Glory Himself had laid and kindled a fire. When all the disciples were gathered together, Jesus called for fish and soon He prepared and cooked a nourishing meal. To those hungry yet joyful men, Jesus issued His gracious invitation: *Come and eat (John 21:12)*.

It is this same gracious invitation that rings down the corridor of two millenniums. Morning by morning, Jesus the Lord stands on the shores of eternity, still inviting us to partake of a heavenly meal that He has carefully prepared. Yes, it is God Himself, Jesus our Lord and Savior, who has meticulously prepared each daily meal for us. It is food for our faith; it is the Word of God; it is the Bible.

In a moment or two, I will invite you to 'listen in' as I turn to the Word to engage in my *Together Time*. I record this personal prayer time **only** because it could prove to be a practical encouragement and invaluable help to you as you regularly respond to your Master's gracious invitation to 'come and eat.' From two entirely different sources I have been prompted to share a real-life *Together Time* with you.

First: A friend of mine who kindly read the script of the previous chapters urged me to do this as a fitting conclusion to this book.

Second: From time to time, over a period of many years, I have been privileged to witness how God has blessed people in a special way when I have led different groups and churches in a collective *Together Time*.

On such occasions, any person present could take part; no questions were to be asked except in silent prayer to the Holy Spirit; and no sermons were to be preached! We commenced each time of fellowship by praying together that the Holy Spirit would be our Teacher. Then in unison we would read aloud the selected Scripture passage. After that, we would return to the beginning of that Scripture passage and together we would again read aloud the first verse. Before proceeding to the next verse, we would have a thirty-second period of silence. During that quiet time, each person would prayerfully meditate upon the verse we had just read to determine if any of the questions which are listed after this chapter could be answered from that verse. Following the silent period of prayer and meditation, each person was free to share with the congregation how the Holy Spirit had applied that verse to his or her heart. This would then be followed with a prayer of response, either by the person who had shared, or by some other member of the congregation.

Incidentally, I believe that this method is the most profitable way to conduct a collective *Together*

***Time*. At this time, I would also urge the readers who are using this book in a group study, to set aside several further meetings for the purpose of applying the above suggestions. [For further help, questions are provided on page 154.]**

The idea of a collective *Together Time* was first introduced to me by the late Thomas B. Rees, a British evangelist, at the Young People's Holiday Conference Centre, where I was converted to Christ. The questions Tom asked for us to answer were a variation of the ones already suggested in the chapter *Together Time*.

Over the long years since then, many of the meetings I have conducted in this way have been accompanied by an unusual sense of God's presence and by the Holy Spirit's speaking to hearts and lives. After such a service at a downtown Baptist church in Victoria, Canada, the pastor remarked, "That was the most blessed and remarkable service I have ever attended during the course of my entire ministry."

Likewise, after several days of services in a Christian & Missionary Alliance Church for Arabs in the Old City of Jerusalem (during which time I spent some of the days teaching these precepts and the other days conducting collective *Together Times*), the retired principal of the Canadian Bible College, who was then living in that ancient city, remarked: "We have never been so close to a real spiritual breakthrough here in Jerusalem!"

In church meetings, home fellowships, Bible conferences, and youth fellowships, God has singularly blessed this public, yet at the same time personal, approach to the Word of God.

I would like to mention, however, that as I attempted to write down my personal *Together Time*, I discovered that it is much more difficult to catch the reality, the glow and the inspiration of my time of personal fellowship with the Lord in print, than it is to experience such a delight privately or even in a public gathering.

To help me record for you the following highlights of my time together with the Lord today, I set myself a few ground rules!

First: I have not let myself select one of my favorite and most familiar passages of the Bible! In my daily *Together Times*, I am reading Paul's Second Epistle to the Corinthians.

Second: The following record of today's portion of Scripture is not intended to be a verse by verse exposition.

Third: To make this account of my *Together Time* as natural (supernatural) as possible, I will share with you the verses that the Holy Spirit has today made living to my heart.

Fourth: I will share with you how God's voice was brought into personal focus when I prayerfully meditated upon God's Word by using some of the questions already suggested.

As I share my meditations with you, you will understand that any *Together Time* is an intensely personal experience. I am aware that your circumstances today are not the same as mine. I am also aware that my circumstances today are not what they will be in six months' time. In His great love, God meets us and speaks to us just where we are, not where we have been, nor where we will be, nor where somebody else is, but where we are! When you read the following record you will be facing totally different circumstances from me. Because God **will** speak to you in relation to your own needs and circumstances, you are personally and daily given your own invitation by the Lord to come and dine.

Surely the Bible is not only God's **living** and **powerful** Word to our hearts, but it is also His **personal** Word to each of us! *For the word of God is living, and powerful . . .* **and is a discerner of the thoughts and intents of the heart** *(Hebrews 4:12).* What could be more personal than that?

In my Bible meditation today, I am reading from the New King James Version. Now, I invite you to listen in as I open my Bible to 2 Corinthians, chapter 1. Please open your own Bible with me.

It is 5:00 a.m.—I have closed my door and opened my Bible to be alone with God.

Some of the circumstances that surround my life today as I come into the presence of God with an open Bible and an open heart are:

- I am particularly concerned about the constant and increasing pain that Dorothy endures. It has become much more severe in these past weeks.

- I am also concerned whether or not her health condition should be a determining factor in finalizing plans for our itinerary of ministry this autumn. So often in the past when I have seen Dorothy suffer in most unusual ways because of our long, demanding missionary journeys, I have said to her, "Dorothy, I will never expose you to this kind of situation again." But then, in one way or another, God has poured out His blessing upon our united ministry, and together we have said, "It has been so gloriously worthwhile!" What about this time, Lord?

- Weighing heavily upon my heart today is the situation in Kenya, where God has been pleased to bless our ministry in the past. The entire situation in that land is extremely unstable, with inflation running rampant. I wish we could do more for the many nationals who are faithfully serving Christ there.

- There are family members on both Dorothy's side and mine who either have been prematurely bereaved or are terminally ill. Because of our complicated and sometimes unpredictable schedules, and because of Dorothy's chronic and severe physical limitations, we seem so inadequate in being able to let them know in practical terms how much we care for them.

Prayer
Father, this morning I praise You for waking me unusually early. I believe that Your purpose was not only that You desire to speak to my heart in a special way, but also that You desire to bless each person who will later

listen in to the time we share together when they hear what You have to say to me through Your Word.

You know, dear Lord, that I do not find it easy to put those people who will later read this record out of my mind in order that I may be conscious only of You. Therefore, in a very special way I pray that You will anoint my heart, my mind and my pencil with transparency, reality and with a real sense of personal intimacy with You.

I affirm again in Your presence that my life is hidden with Christ in God. Thank You for such a wonderful assurance. I also praise You, dear Lord, that, even though the record I am writing with my hands here on earth might be sadly biased by my own personal perspective, in Heaven You are my Great High Priest and will present my prayers and praise before the Father's throne according to Your perfect knowledge and will. So with glad anticipation I turn to Your Word this morning. Open my eyes this day that I may behold wondrous things in Your Word.

Dear Reader, today, I turn to 2 Corinthians, chapter 1, and then slowly read aloud through the entire chapter. I do this with a distinct voice and with no prolonged pauses. I invite you to do the same.

When a moment or two ago I read the chapter in this way, I became very conscious of Paul's exemplary conduct as a servant of Christ. Now it is apparent to me that much of my time with the Lord today will answer the question: **Is there in this verse an example to follow?**

From my first reading of the entire chapter, already my heart has been inclined by the Holy Spirit to follow Paul's noble examples. I do want to be a better servant of my Lord. Before I proceed to meditate verse by verse through the chapter, I will tell Him so.

Prayer

Lord Jesus, I sincerely want to be able to reflect upon my life of service to You with similar satisfaction that I sense in the testimony of Paul that I have just read. In a thousand ways You have poured out Your blessings in my life and I am sad to acknowledge that all too often it has been a one-way street. My heart grows weary of sincerely expressing my desire to fellowship with You, but then, when You give me opportunity to share the fellowship of Your sufferings, I flinch like a coward. As I am

about to meditate upon these verses again,
please overshadow me with Your presence
and Your power and touch my life afresh in a
life-transforming way so that my selfish habit
patterns may be permanently and radically
changed for Your own dear Name's sake.

Now, I will return and read the same chapter
verse by verse and thought by thought. As I do so, I
will continually pray that the Holy Spirit may not let
me miss the message that God wants to convey to my
heart in answer to my prayer. In this manner, my
two-way conversation with God will begin. I also
remind myself that as I meditate upon each verse I
must be careful not to hurry past any verse that I am
already familiar with. Today, God may want to make
that verse living to my heart in a new and special
way. So I ask: **Is there in this passage a fresh thought
about God the Father?**

Reading
Verse 3: *The Father of mercies, and God of all comfort.*

Today, I particularly notice that this statement
about the Fatherhood of God is preceded by another
reference to God's Fatherhood found in verse 2. As I
looked at my marginal reference, I read that verse 2
could be translated: *The God and Father of our Lord*

Jesus Christ. Just think of it: the God and Father of the Lord Jesus Christ is also my Father of *mercy* and *comfort.* For my comfort, my Father in Heaven has extended His Grace and Peace to me.

Prayer

Father, I bow before You with thanksgiving and praise. I thank You for Your 'Grace.' You have extended to my heart that which is eternally Yours—Your 'Peace!' Through Your grace—the peace, the tranquillity, the harmony that has forever existed in who You are, are mine today! Hallelujah! By Your Holy Spirit, minister to my ruffled heart, I pray. As I bow in Your holy presence, fill my life with the quietness and the peace of Your own indwelling, I pray.

Reading

Verse 4: *Who comforts us in all our tribulation, that we may be able to comfort those who are in any trouble, with the comfort with which we ourselves are comforted by God.*

As I meditate upon this testimony of Paul's, I notice some other words that he used in the context of the 'comfort' that he had received from his Heavenly Father. They are: 'tribulation', 'afflicted', 'trouble', 'sufferings' and 'sentence of death.' The Holy Spirit seems to be drawing my attention to the fact that these experiences are far removed from the usual concept of 'comfort.'

As I read on, I notice that Paul also testified that all the difficulties of life are permitted by God for one specific purpose: *that we should not trust in ourselves, but in God who raises the dead.* I also observe from verse 4 that the reason God ministered His comfort to Paul was not that he should be comfortable but that he should be a comforter of others. I must pray this one through!

Prayer

Yes Lord, You know the times in my life when I have sincerely wanted to bring comfort and consolation to hurting people. I have so wanted to minister Your comfort to Dorothy as she suffers so constantly and intensely in her body.

All too often, I seem to take so much from her and so seldom do I minister Your grace and peace for her comfort and consolation. Please forgive my selfish ways and fill me afresh with a desire to serve and not be served.

And, as I also think of the millions of hurting people who live in desolate and difficult conditions where hunger and disease and death prevail, I pray that Your grace and peace will be so magnified in my heart and that Your presence will be so evident in my life that it will be used to lift burdens from others and to comfort those people who live in such dreadful conditions.

But even as I pray, Lord Jesus, I understand more clearly how Your comfort attends each difficulty of life no matter how severe, and that it is allowed by Your loving heart that I might not trust in myself but in You.

Now at this very point, the Word of God is becoming penetratingly powerful to me. I realize that even Paul was ministered to by a somber list of difficulties to strip him of self-confidence. Why then, should I complain if, in His love, God chooses to answer my prayer by allowing perplexity and adversity to deal with my pride?

Prayer

Yes, Lord, I want to thank You for Your ministry of love in my life. Though it is difficult to record this prayer for other people to read, I am encouraged that Paul was transparent about his severe trials before those whom he loved. He did not confine his testimony to the good things of life, so from the bottom of my heart today I will praise You for every lonely moment in my service to You, for every heartache You have allowed to come my way, for every time I have been misunderstood, for every foolish and sinful blunder of my life, for every overwhelming circumstance when I failed because I trusted in my own self and not in You. Now, Lord Jesus, in Your Holy Presence, I affirm with Paul that I will not trust in myself but in You.

Lord, only the other day I read Paul's words: our sufficiency is of God. *This morning I affirm by faith that You and You alone are my sufficiency. Dear Lord, in the words of Scripture that are open before me, I praise* You— *that **You have** delivered me; and that **You do** deliver me; and that **You will** yet deliver me— from myself! Thank **You** Lord Jesus, for such a great salvation!*

Now, Lord, as the Holy Spirit strengthens my heart with Your comfort, I expectantly ask You to use me in practical and loving ways today, to bring Your comfort and help to people I might meet today who need Your love.'

Reading
Verse 11: *You also helping together in prayer for us . . . by many persons.*

I wonder what Paul's ministry would have been like if many faces had not been lifted up to God on his behalf. Likewise, I wonder where I would be today if it were not for my many friends who *help together in prayer*.

Prayer

Father, I cannot comprehend Your great love to me in that You have laid it upon the heart of so many of Your dear children to pray for Dorothy and me. How can I express my thanks to You for such wondrous love?

Now, I specifically commit some of these friends to God in a time of intercessory prayer. As I do so, I try to pray for them in the light of the Scriptures that the Holy Spirit has been impressing upon my own heart and life, asking that God bring His own comfort (strength) to their hearts and lives as they totally put their trust in Him.*

Reading

Verses 15, 17-18: *I intended to come to you before . . . do I plan according to the flesh? . . . our word to you was not yes and no.*

I meditate upon this sequence of thought. Paul testified that his only concern to go to Corinth the second time was to minister 'comfort' and 'consolation' and 'benefit' to the saints whom he loved. He did not desire to go there to receive from them; on the contrary, he wanted to give to them.

He also testified that he had not made his travel plans lightly. (I notice there is no mention of who would pay his travel expenses and money played no part in his going!) Certainly, personal advantage played no part in his decision to go to Corinth.

Prayer

*By Your Spirit, and through Your Word, dear Lord, show me any wrong motive in my heart that would quench the working of Your Holy Spirit when I determine what is your will as to where I should minister this coming autumn. It seems to me Lord, that, even though the Christians at Corinth misconstrued Paul's motives when he made the unusual decision to change his travel plans, he was persuaded only by the leading of Your Spirit. But, thank You, Lord, that although Paul said yes and then had changed his response to no for his itinerary, the Word he preached was never **yes** and then **no**, for in Christ it is always **yes**, unchanged and eternal. There are no changes in Your Heart, Lord; the Word of God that Paul preached is eternally verified by You. Thank You, Lord, for being this solid rock in my world—in my world where circumstances shift so quickly,*

---

* Please turn to page 156 and 157 for further suggestions to help you in intercessory prayer.

where plans must be made and sometimes changed. Lord, I need to know Your plans. Save me from decisions that flow from expediency or opportunism. Let me walk in fellowship with You each day, I pray.

Reading

Verse 20: *For all the promises of God in Him* [Christ] *are Yes, and in Him Amen, to the Glory of God **through us**.*

As I observe that God's promises are made personal "through us," I ask: **Is there in this passage a promise for me to claim?**

Prayer

***Through us,** Lord? The promises of God— through us! The promises of God **in Christ?** All the promises of God in Christ, Lord? Yes, Lord, thank You. This morning in Your Holy Presence I want to record my own yes and amen to that, Lord! O God, I cannot conceive of **all** that **You** have given me **in Christ**. Indeed, I cannot imagine how empty my life would be without You, dear Lord. Today, Lord Jesus, I affirm that You are all I need as I face the demands of today with all its opportunities, its testings and its decisions.*

I now spend some time worshiping and praising my Lord as His peace floods my soul. I do not know the specific answers to my prayer requests, but that does not really matter, for I have the peace of God in my heart. I have spent invaluable *Together Time* with my Lord. Praise Him! Now, as I go into today, God has given me precious food from His Word upon which my mind and heart can reflect when I will later be faced with the demands of the day.

So, let us constantly remember, the foremost and primary duty that to which each one of us must attend every morning is to "get our soul in a happy state before God."

How wonderful to know that every day the Lord Jesus extends His very own personal invitation to you. Calling you by name, He graciously invites *you* to ***Come and Dine***!

> Thy truth unchanged hath ever stood;
> Thou savest those that on Thee call;
> To them that seek Thee Thou art good;
> To them that find Thee, All in All.
>
> We taste Thee, O Thou Living Bread,
> And long to feast upon Thee still;
> We drink of Thee, the Fountainhead,
> And Thirst our souls from Thee to fill.
>
> Bernard of Clairvaux

Note. Though a formal Bible study is not absolutely vital every day, a daily *Together Time* is imperative for your spiritual growth.

Bible Study

Here are some questions for you to ask in relation to the Bible passages you will read, so that you will truly have a rewarding formal Bible Study:

Of whom is the passage speaking?

To whom is the passage directed?

What specific words does the writer use?

At what time was the passage written?

From where was the passage written?

For what purpose was the passage written?

In what situation was the passage written?

How does the passage fit into what goes before it and what follows it?

Be diligent to present yourself approved to God as a workman who does not need to be ashamed, handling accurately the word of truth (2 Timothy 2:15 NASB).

Together Time

Here are some questions for you to ask as you meditate on each verse in your daily reading of the Scripture:

Is there in this verse a:

Sin to avoid?

Warning to heed?

Command to obey?

Good example to follow?

Bad example to shun?

New thought about God the Father?

New thought about God the Son?

New thought about God the Holy Spirit?

Fresh insight into the person of Satan?

Fresh insight into Satan's cruel goals?

Fresh insight into Satan's subtle devices?

But be ye doers of the word and not hearers only, deceiving your own selves. But whosoever looketh into the perfect law of liberty, and continueth in it, he being not a forgetful hearer but a doer of the word, this man shall be blessed in his deed (James 1:22,25 KJ).

DAILY PRAYER GUIDE

To help my wife Dorothy and me in our daily intercessory prayer, we have sought to follow the daily sequence which was first suggested by Evangelist Thomas B. Rees just after I was converted to Christ over 50 years ago. M for Monday; M for missionaries and so on.

Having already fed our souls on God's word and prayed it from head to heart, supplicatory prayer becomes vitalized. Instead of a perfunctory daily routine, supplication for others becomes a protracted and fresh time of thanksgiving, intercession and concern for them. Though we do not have a documented list of prayer concerns in this way, we trust the Holy Spirit to expand our prayer time to embrace all immediate prayer needs whatever they may be.

Be anxious for nothing, but in everything by prayer and supplication, with thanksgiving, let your requests be made known to God (Phil. 4:6).

Note: The following **Daily Prayer Guide** does not exclude praying for concerns of a personal nature or that may arise on a daily basis.